A
Time
to
Listen

A
Time
to
Listen

by
Patricia
Hermes

PREVENTING
YOUTH
SUICIDE

HARCOURT BRACE JOVANOVICH, PUBLISHERS
SAN DIEGO   NEW YORK   LONDON

Requests for permission to make copies of any
part of this work should be mailed to:
Permissions Department, Harcourt Brace Jovanovich, Publishers,
Orlando, Florida 32887.

All interviews in this book are based on actual interviews with real people.
Due to the sensitivity of the material, names and other identifying characteristics have been changed to protect the privacy of those involved.

Library of Congress Cataloging-in-Publication Data
Hermes, Patricia.
   A time to listen.
   Includes index.
   1. Youth — United States — Suicidal behavior — Case
studies. 2. Suicide — United States — Prevention — Case
studies. I. Title.
HV6546.H46 1987   362.2   87-12021
ISBN 0-15-288196-4

Designed by Janet S. Taggart
Printed in the United States of America

B C D E F

For those who shared with me their private inner worlds.
And especially for my children—

Paul, Mark, Tim, Matthew, and Jennifer.

CONTENTS

Contents

A
Time
to
Listen

Chapter 1

Introduction

A Time to Listen

Although for several years I, like most people, had become aware of the upsurge in teen suicide, I somehow believed that those who were dying were not ordinary young people coping with ordinary life crises. They were, I told myself, the dropouts, the ones involved with drugs, the sad, alienated youth. It was a reassuring falsehood. It was not that I felt indifferent or callous toward those in that kind of pain; I just felt safe. Until the year when just about every month another young friend of mine or of my children died or attempted to die by his or her own hand. And these *were* seemingly "normal, ordinary" kids. These weren't runaways, or dropouts, or young people crazed with drugs. I knew. I had known them. Then why? I asked myself. What made apparently normal, healthy young people decide to end their lives? What kind of pain or fear was driving them? It was clear I could no longer con myself into believing the comfortable lie—that "ordinary" kids were immune to this tragedy.

Was *anyone* immune? I did not know, but both as a mother and as a writer, I knew I needed to research, I needed to find out, and I needed to write about it. As I did, I found new concerns: My children were deeply saddened by the suicides and attempted suicides of their friends. I worried that suicide could become "contagious."

Then I became aware of several recent studies that seemed to show a correlation between an upsurge in teen suicides, and television accounts—both real and fictional— of other teen suicides. Could it be that talking about suicide, reading about it, seeing it on TV could actually *cause* the phenomenon? Would we all be better off keeping quiet about it, putting it back in the closet?

I put this question to respected professionals, whose consensus was that news accounts of teen suicides, as well as books and movies and TV, are not themselves the problems. There is a problem, however. That problem, according to many experts, is the *sensationalizing* of teen suicide.

Dr. Pamela Cantor, President of the American Association of Suicidology, Cochairperson of the National Committee on Youth Suicide Prevention, and a respected authority on teen suicide, says that teens are looking for heroes, role models. She suggests that when a hero in a TV drama uses suicide as a way to solve problems, there *is* some danger that disturbed viewers might follow. However, that is not a reason to avoid discussing suicide in a rational, instructional way. To say, "If you tell kids about suicide they will do it," she claims, is about as reasonable as saying, "If you tell kids about herpes they will go out and get it."

In fact, according to Dr. Cantor and other experts, while sensationalism must be scrupulously avoided in TV as well as in newspapers and books, it is not *education* about suicide that is harmful; it is *ignorance.*

Even knowing that, why write one more book on the problem of youth suicide? Why give young people more facts, when they have all the facts they'll ever need? They already know how many of their friends are dying. They don't need to be reminded of the numbers, nor do they need to be told how it feels to be left behind. They also know all about despair. And when in the depths of that despair and seriously thinking of ending his/her own life, will any one of them really stop to read a book? What could one possibly say that would make a difference?

For my whole adult writing life, I have labored to give young people the words they need. But on the subject of suicide, it began to seem that young people had all the words they'd ever need.

What was needed now was someone who would listen. Listen? How could one listen in a book?

I went out with my tape recorder. I talked to young people, those who had direct experience with suicide and were willing to talk. They *wanted* to talk. They *wanted* to be heard. I talked to the parents of young people who had died. I talked to their friends and their therapists.

I listened, and I learned that had enough people been listening sooner, some tragic events might never have happened. I listened to teens who themselves had contemplated or attempted suicide, and I learned that all the warning signs of an impending suicide attempt were often—not always, but often—clearly spelled out for the rest of us to hear. I learned, from talking to friends of those who died, that some things could be changed—and some could not. From parents of young people who had died, I heard the most urgent pleas to the young to listen. However, I also learned that someone who is really intent on killing himself cannot always be stopped, and this is an important point to know.

Most important, I learned that an eager, willing listening to those involved in their own life-and-death struggles could change things for other young people. Yes, the research is important—and facts are certainly included in this book. But it's become, I hope, not a book to give answers, but a book that, having given people a chance to talk—young people, their parents, their psychiatrists—will now give others a chance to listen.

I am deeply indebted to those who agreed to be interviewed for this book. They spoke freely, openly, and with enormous courage and honesty. Their views are their own, and as such, subjective—for none of them claimed to be all-knowing. For clarity and continuity, as well as information and objectivity, these interviews have been edited and further commentary supplied where necessary. Small parts of one interview were supplemented by some original writings of the interviewee.

All names have been changed, with the exception of the therapist in Chapter 9, Dr. Eleanor Craig, and the names of the experts quoted. All interviews include material that has been deliberately altered to protect the privacy of the individuals.

And so this book. One that I hope may help some, young or old, to plow onward, to get through the tough times, to continue to seek a path—not to annihilation—but to the future.

Chapter 2

Interview with Kelly O'Connor, Part 1

Myths about Suicide
The Danger of Seeing No Options
Stresses Unique to Teens
Where to Turn for Help

I open this book with an interview with Kelly O'Connor, who just a few years ago, when she was a junior in high school, made some very serious plans to kill herself. I chose Kelly first, not only because she is so verbal, so clear about herself and her motives, but also because in some ways Kelly is such a "typical" teenager. She's bright. She has friends. She is not a loner in the usual sense of the word although, like many teens and adults, she is sometimes lonely. She's had her share of problems at home and at school—rather ordinary problems that many adolescents deal with. She's attractive and outgoing and vivacious and caring.

During the period of her sadness and depression, Kelly was showing all the classic signs of one who is about to make a lethal attempt on her life. And she was bright enough to know exactly what she was doing—and to be able to tell us. This quality of clarity and awareness makes Kelly's interview outstanding.

The interview with Kelly dispels many of the myths about suicide—that talking about suicide causes suicide, that the person who talks about suicide does not intend to do it (frequently, the one who talks about it *does* do it), that only sick, crazy people kill themselves. Kelly educates us not by lecturing, but by her experience. In addition, she is so intelligent—and so lucky to get through her experience—that she is able to say, in her words, and with exceptional forcefulness to others like her: If you see anyone else doing what I was doing, sending out the signals I was sending, do something for that person. These are the clear warning signs of an impending suicide attempt. Do for them what I wish someone had done for me.

Perhaps the most important reason for beginning with Kelly is her statement: "I don't believe that anyone who thinks about or feels like committing suicide really wants to die. It's just a matter of not wanting to live life as it is right then, and not seeing . . . other options. It's either life or death. And kids see it as life *as it is*."

Kelly is proof that life can change, and that one does not have to *die* in order to change things. Kelly sought and received psychological help, and was admitted for a time to a psychiatric hospital. She is now enrolled in college, and her career goal is to help other troubled teens.

———

In the following, Q represents me as the questioner, K is Kelly, and **Dr. Cheryl Skowronski** is fully identified the few times she speaks. Dr. Skowronski is a minister and counselor at the Silver Point Presbyterian Church in Greenville, North Carolina. I had read that she was conducting group meetings to help teenagers deal with their suicidal urges. Kelly was a member of that group. They both agreed to be interviewed, and the following conversation took place. These are not their true names.

Dr. Skowronski's first project was a support group for widows and widowers. From families whose loved ones had committed suicide, however, there came a request for Dr. Skowronski to form a separate group. They felt that their problems were different, and their guilt was much different. It was then that Kelly came on the scene with a new idea: You're putting the cart before the horse—you should have a group for those who've been *thinking* of suicide. Dr. Skowronski checked around and found that there were no such groups outside of hospitals. Having seen the need, "we attempted to fill it," Dr. Skowronski says. But once again, from that group, it became obvious that teenagers with suicidal feelings are different from adults with the same feelings.

Q: Kelly, how are the problems for teens different from the problems of adults who also may be coping with despair?

K: Well, one of the biggest problems is that a lot of adults don't understand the perspective of adolescents. They tend to downplay our problems. Compared to paying bills or paying the mortgage or trying to keep a roof over their heads, our problems seem so much smaller. But to teenagers who don't have to deal with an adult's problems, their problems *are* big problems. Friends, boyfriends, girlfriends, school, work, family—family can be a *big* one. A lot of adolescents don't identify with their families, and that's hard for the families to understand. Kids tend to want to spend more time with their friends. They get tired of family vacations, and that kind of thing.

Q: Could you talk about what drove you to the point

7

of wanting to make an attempt on your life? Did you really want to die?

K: No. I don't believe that anyone who thinks about or feels like committing suicide really wants to die. It's just a matter of not wanting to live life as it is right then, and not seeing another alternative. It's hard to see any other options. It's either life or death. And kids see it as life *as it is*.

Q: So you didn't want to die, but you didn't want to live the way things were. So what you were hoping to accomplish, maybe, was change?

K: Yes. I think in a lot of circumstances it's the only way for teenagers to *say* that they can't go on living the way things are. It's a very hard thing—when you're feeling that way—to put it into words or to ask somebody for help. It's something a teenager probably hasn't experienced before—the feeling that you want to kill yourself. And to feel like killing yourself—well, it's a hard thing to go up to your parents (who by this point you don't really identify with anyway—or at least, I didn't) and say, "Hey, I feel like killing myself, I think I need to see a psychiatrist." It's a really strange thing to say, with all the stigma in our society about psychiatrists. It's just a very difficult thing to put into words to your parents.

Q: Especially when parents may be part of the problem?

K: Yes. So I didn't tell them. My way of getting the message across to them was to tell a friend of mine who I knew would talk to a teacher in school, and then I knew the message would get to my parents that way.

Q: So you think that if a young person is telling friends, then that's really a way of asking for help—what's really being said is "help me, do something"?

K: Definitely. And I don't believe that anyone really

wants to die at that point. They just don't know that another way exists, that there is another way of *changing* their lives. They don't see that. So, they're hoping that someone will stop them, and that someone who *knows* how to change things will be able to help them.

Q: Someone who knows how?

K: A psychiatrist or something. But they don't know who at that point. I didn't know. But I *did* know that I'd need to be put in a hospital—when I got to a certain point. It was very frightening—very hard to put into words. The day after I decided I was definitely going to kill myself, I went into school and I was talking to the nurse, who was a friend of mine, and I was in a very good mood. I was ecstatic. My problems were going to be over! But a part of me was saying: This is not right, something's wrong here. I was hoping that my friends would pick up on it. A sudden change in mood is supposed to be one of the big signs, a sign that someone who has been really depressed may be about to kill herself. And so I was hoping my friends would pick up on it. But they didn't; even my best friend misunderstood. So I went and talked to the school nurse, and I was kind of beating around the bush and dropping hints, and I realized *she* wasn't going to pick up on it either. And so I came right out and told her. She called my psychiatrist, and they went back and forth and back and forth and basically, at that point, I ended up needing to be put in a hospital.

Q: So you were already seeing a psychiatrist?

K: Yes.

Q: But it wasn't helping?

K: No. In fact, it was really after my last appointment with that psychiatrist that I definitely decided to kill myself.

Q: That must have been really scary—not getting the right kind of help from your own doctor.

Dr. Skowronski: Why don't you tell her what the psychiatrist said—it might be helpful to know what *not* to say.

K: Well, I can't remember exactly what happened in that last session. But next day when I talked to the school nurse, she called my doctor and explained to her that I was really upset. Then the nurse handed the phone to me. And the doctor told me that I wasn't strong enough to kill myself. I was sitting there mouthing, "Just you watch me." I had my fists clenched; I was ready to get up and hit something. I handed the phone back to the nurse, and she grabbed my arm. She had read my lips when I was mouthing "just you watch me." She told my doctor that she didn't think that what she had just said had really helped. They talked a while longer, and the phone was handed back to me. And that's when my doctor said, "Now I'm going to have to put you in the hospital, now that you've upset the school nurse." I thought that was a *great* reason to hospitalize somebody! So—

Q: I hope you found another doctor?

K: Oh, I did! When I went to the hospital I found a very good psychiatrist there. It worked out very well for me. I think it's very hard, with your first psychiatrist, to realize that he or she is not the only one out there. You think: Maybe I should trust this person, she knows what she's doing—I'm really uncomfortable with her, but she *is* the professional. But there are all sorts of different techniques. And if you don't click with one, it doesn't necessarily mean that it's you. It could just be that the relationship is wrong. I went through three weeks with that first one, and she ended up basically daring me to kill myself. Till that point, I really hadn't given much thought to finding someone else, even though I left some of the sessions feeling that nothing had been accomplished. It had been a lot of talk that went nowhere. For instance, I saw her twice a week for three weeks, and we spent one of those forty-five-minute sessions playing chess.

———

Although Kelly mentions a "stigma" attached to seeing a psychiatrist, and some biases and problems with her first psychiatrist, these problems were uniquely her own. Very few people today feel that there is a stigma attached to getting counseling or psychiatric care. And fortunately, many people are able to relate to the first therapist with whom they work. What is important to recognize, however, is what Kelly eventually recognized—that just as there are many different kinds of individuals, there are many different kinds of therapists and therapeutic techniques to choose from. What works well with one individual may not work with another. But one must begin somewhere because a good therapist, one who understands the needs of a sad or depressed youth, can be an invaluable influence in turning one's thoughts from death to life. How to begin? Choose a therapist—a recommendation from a friend is an ideal place to start (see Chapter 3 for more information)—but remain flexible. If it's clear that a relationship is not forming between you and the therapist, find someone else with whom you do feel comfortable.

In addition, besides psychiatrists (who are medical doctors trained to deal with the emotions) and psychologists (who are also trained in dealing with emotions, but are not medical doctors nor licensed to prescribe drugs), there are many other kinds of counselors—social workers, guidance counselors, etc. Also, a minister, priest, or rabbi can often be helpful as a counselor. The word of caution here is that although many clergy are well qualified to help those suffering with a temporary emotional problem, not all are thoroughly qualified to deal with a long-term problem or with a crisis. Most clergy will be honest in telling the individual if further help is needed from a different kind of therapist. Many people feel comfortable beginning with their familiar clergy. If nothing else, it is sometimes a very good place to start.

Q: Could you talk now about why you felt so bad, or what led up to the crisis?

K: A lot of things built up to it, some of which, two years later, I'm just beginning to work on. I grew up holding in all my feelings—anger, for instance. Tears. I didn't cry. After I was about five years old, I cried very little if at all. Never with my family. I would cry with my cat—he was my best friend. He was the only one I talked to about my problems.

Q: That sounds so lonely. A cat doesn't talk back.

K: Yes, but I liked that, given the alternative of talking to my family and having them respond in a way that just made me angrier or more upset. If he didn't respond, at least he didn't increase the bad feelings. So I could kind of believe that he understood.

In grade school, I had very few friends. I was very much a loner. I got very good grades. I used to spend about seven hours a night on homework. When I wasn't doing homework, I was watching television. There was even a period of time when I didn't eat with the family. I'd sit downstairs and watch TV while I was eating my dinner. When I hit high school, I started making friends and having fun. I didn't need to work as hard, because I'd gone to a good grade school and I'd learned a lot of things they were teaching in the freshman year. My second year, I had some problems getting along with my best friend, and my grades slipped a little bit—down to C's in a few of my classes. And then junior year, they took a nose dive. I failed chemistry first quarter, and was able to get a doctor's note to get out of classes. I didn't like chemistry and I wasn't interested in it, but failing really upset me. I had so much on my mind—problems with school, anger at my family—but more than that, just this sad, sad feeling that felt so awful. I got out of that class, but then about mid-year everything went— D's, F's.

Q: You couldn't concentrate? Or didn't care?

K: No, I just didn't even *know* it was happening. I wasn't in the habit of keeping track of my grades and figuring out what my grades would be at the end of the quarter. I'd get a bad paper, and figure, well, it was behind me now, there wasn't anything I could do about it. So I wasn't even expecting the bad grades. And my parents just freaked out. For the first time in my life, they grounded me. I could only go to school or to work. And only fifteen minutes on the phone, which really limited the contact I could have with my friends. And at that point, my friends were the only thing that was keeping me alive.

Q: Was it a specific thing that was wrong then? Something that you knew and could identify?

K: More than anything, it was just this huge sadness. This huge, huge sad feeling inside. I began feeling more and more depressed. Later, my parents told me that they had grounded me not so much to punish me, but to keep an eye on me, because they knew that something was wrong for my grades to go like that. But they were angry at me, and yelling, and giving me a hard time, and it was so hard to deal with. It was just a few weeks later—maybe not even a few weeks—that I started talking about suicide to my friends.

Q: But not to your parents?

K: No. I was always very good at putting on an act around them. Inside, I could be so upset that I was about to fall apart, but I'd walk in that front door and the smile would go on—nothing's wrong, no problems, not upset, not angry!" That kind of acting was something I'd been doing for seventeen years. So they didn't really know anything was going on. But finally I was getting to the point where I wanted help. I knew I was getting too close to doing something.

Q: Like what?

K: I would have OD'd. I had it all planned out. Pain-killers, aspirin. I was always the last one to bed, so I'd take them right before I went to bed, and no one would be missing me till six o'clock in the morning. I figured by then it would be too late. I started talking to my friends about it, and they were getting worried.

Q: Why were you telling your friends? Did you want them to stop you?

K: Yes. I didn't know who to ask for help. I didn't know who could help me, who could make the pain go away. But I was hoping that maybe by telling my friends, the word would get out to someone who could get in there and help me. Finally my best friend, Andrea, talked to one of my teachers about it, and the teacher had Andrea talk to the school nurse. That day at lunch, I was called up to the administration office. This woman from the office came down and walked with me to the administration office, and she didn't say a word to me the whole time. I walked in, and there were my parents and Andrea and the nurse. I sat down between my mother and Andrea—I would really rather just have been sitting next to Andrea—and they started talking about it. It was after that that I began seeing my first psychiatrist.

Q: So you were allowed to continue in school after that—home and school, life as usual? As long as you were seeing a psychiatrist?

K: Yes, because at that point, I was able to say to the psychiatrist that I wasn't about to do anything to hurt myself.

Q: And mean it?

K: Yes.

Q: But it was only three weeks later that you felt desperate enough to make plans again?

K: Yes. I wish I could remember what we discussed in that last session. I remember driving home from that session with my arms straight out, pushing my back into the back of the driver's seat, and having to fight to keep my foot up on the accelerator—having to fight to keep it from jamming down.

But when I got home, the smile went on: "No problems! The appointment was fine!" I went to my room. At that point, I was getting home-bound assignments—the school was letting me get my work done at my own pace. And that's when my own pace was not at all, so the assignments just weren't getting done. I had been given two weeks to do them, and now it was the end of the two weeks. I was in my room, staring at my books, and I felt like throwing them out the window, or running away from them, or just getting away.

And that's when I decided that the only way out was to get out. It's going to be over! I thought. All my problems are going to be over! And I believe in heaven. And even though it's probably a sin to kill yourself, well, I believed that if you killed yourself, it was because you had gotten to the point where you couldn't handle it. There was something emotionally wrong, you weren't thinking straight. And I figured God wouldn't blame you for that. I figured that the people who loved me would have to understand that I was hurting too bad to go on and that now I wasn't hurting anymore. So I rationalized: Great, my problems will be over and I'll get to go to heaven. Had written a poem about it. So I was ecstatic. Really happy. Went to bed happy.

But it was the next day that I went into school—hoping that someone would pick up on what was happening to me. And ended up telling the nurse who would stop me.

———

" . . . *the nurse who would stop me.*"

Kelly was begging someone to stop her. But she didn't know where to turn. Or to whom. Friends? The school nurse? The psychiatrist with whom she was not relating well? She even briefly mentions religion.

It is important to mention here that while religion is sometimes a solace for people in time of trouble, for some others, including those who are contemplating suicide, the strictures of church teaching may carry little weight when they feel desperate with pain. Who can consider a church teaching on suicide when one's mind is perhaps overwhelmed with fear or pain? Or, as in Kelly's case, one in such turmoil can rationalize church teachings to fit one's own particular desperation. Which is perhaps why some religions, while vigorously condemning suicide, now allow church funerals for those who have died from suicide. It is not that suicide is approved as a way of dealing with pain. Rather, a church funeral is an acknowledgment, on the part of those who believe, that only God knows and can judge the final motives and moments of an individual's life.

And so we hear in Kelly's own words that she was looking everywhere for help. She was hurting desperately. She had made some dangerous decisions. She was frantically sending out all the signals. But perhaps most important, at the same time that she was planning her own death, she was also saying, "Stop what I am going to do. Help me. Save me."

Most people in Kelly's situation—probably all people—are saying the same thing, yet saying it without words. "Actions speak louder than words" is the old truism. In the case of contemplated suicide, that is not quite true. The actions say, "I want to die." But the unspoken cry is: "Don't let me do it. Don't let me die. Save me."

Chapter 3

Facts about Suicide

Warning Signs
What Family and Friends Should Do
How to Listen

Kelly was exhibiting many of the signs that the experts say may point to a possible suicide attempt. Yet because she was hurting and confused—and smart—she was able to hide that preoccupation with death and dying on certain days and from certain individuals. On other days (or other hours or even moments), she was deliberately, consciously, sending signals for help. On the one hand she was saying, "I'm all right, no problems, everything's fine." On the other hand she was saying, "I'm not all right, help me."

No wonder, then—with all the conflicting feelings and signals that the individual is sending out—that it is sometimes so difficult to identify and reach out to those in need! For Kelly is not unique. She speaks for many young people in her situation.

Yet almost all professionals would agree that anyone exhibiting even a few of the signs that Kelly did is probably an individual in need and very possibly an individual at risk.

What are the warning signs that an individual is contemplating ending his/her own life?

Not surprisingly, a prime warning signal is preoccupation with the themes of death and dying. Many young people have been known to write poems, stories, essays, and songs about death and suicide shortly before their own self-inflicted deaths. Sometimes these written pages are handed to a teacher or to a close friend. It is a subtle sign, but for the individual on the lookout, it is a telltale one.

Another sign is talking about suicide and the wish to die. *It is a myth that those who talk about suicide won't do it.* Studies have shown that many of those who have killed themselves have given clear indications of their plans in advance, both in word and in action.

Persistent indications that a person feels depressed and sad and hopeless—complaints about feeling worthless and useless.

Giving away loved possessions—record collections, bicycles, a favorite jacket or sweater. When such a gift is presented with a statement like "Here, I won't be needing these much longer," it is often a sign that suicide may be very much in the gift-giver's thoughts. Also, making final arrangements or making a will may be a warning sign.

Changes in sleeping habits—the individual who suddenly can't sleep, or who falls asleep easily, only to awaken after an hour or so and then lie wakeful all night. Similarly, the individual who suddenly seems to be sleeping all the time may be at risk.

Changes in eating habits that are sudden and extreme—a major weight loss or gain, for example. In addition, an inability to eat or a sudden disinterest in food may give a clue that something is wrong.

A major, sudden behavioral or personality change should also alert family and friends to the possibility of trouble. For example, a person who displays sudden apathy, nervousness, outbursts of anger. Or an individual who has previously been outgoing and friendly and who becomes suddenly withdrawn and morose. Conversely, outgoing and vivacious behavior on the part of someone normally shy and withdrawn may also point to an impending suicide. For young people, perhaps the most obvious behavioral change may be someone who has normally taken great pride in her/his appearance, and who suddenly appears not to care. Another, and perhaps more important, clue is the sign of cheerfulness and hope in a person who has recently appeared sad and hopeless. This may well mean that a suicide is imminent—plans have already been made, and the individual feels cheerful because soon the pain will be over.

A sudden change in school performance is also suspect, as is the inability to concentrate or the inability to sit still. Any hobby or activity that is carried to extremes.

Increased use of drugs or alcohol. Most experts say drugs and alcohol don't *cause* suicide, but alcohol and certain drugs are depressants. Use of such substances may increase any depression already present.

Excessive risk-taking. Driving too fast, as well as the lethal combination of drinking and driving, are the more obvious signs of risk-taking. But there are more subtle signs as well. The individual who is constantly injuring him/herself in accidents, or who has frequent falls or broken bones, may well be an individual who is at risk.

Although these are the familiar warning signals, it would be a mistake to say that just because an individual is not exhibiting these particular characteristics, he/she is not in danger. These are generalizations, and there's many a young person who is able to hide trouble and depression under a mask of well-being. If you suspect that something is wrong, it is far better to overreact than to underreact. Remember that talking about suicide doesn't cause suicide. But talking about it to someone who has been thinking about it may give just the opening that he or she has been secretly hoping for.

Other danger signals of a person at risk are less clear perhaps than the foregoing. It is thought by some professionals, for example, that a young person is in more danger than usual if he/she has a friend or loved one who has recently died of or attempted suicide—particularly if it was a parent or sibling. There is no evidence of a *genetic* link to suicide. The link—if one may call it that—may be that the young person has an *example* to follow: My friend (or sister, brother, etc.) died that way; I can, too. Or as one professional counselor put it, it may be a case of "Do unto others as has been done unto me."

Teenagers who have recently suffered a great personal loss—breakup with a boyfriend or girlfriend, for example, or loss of prestige or a goal—getting into the college of one's choice, perhaps. Not everyone who experiences a loss is in danger of suicide, for loss is occasionally a part of everyone's life. But if an individual seems unusually sad or depressed, and in addition has recently suffered a personal loss, that person may very well be at risk.

Finally, anyone who has previously made an attempt on his/her life, no matter how "trivial" that attempt seems—just a "few" pills too many, or some surface slashes on the wrist—anyone who has made any attempt is at much greater risk than the general population.

What, then, can families or friends do if a loved one is exhibiting signs of trouble?

Almost all professionals say one thing first and above

all else: *Get help; and get help with getting more help*. If it's a child, a family would be well advised to find a psychiatrist or psychologist who can be trusted, and with whom the family members feel comfortable. A counselor who is caring and willing to become involved, not only with the individual who is hurting, but also preferably with the entire family, would be an ideal choice.

Seeking out help may seem an obvious step, but it may also seem formidable. When a family is in the midst of a crisis, it takes enormous amounts of energy and thought simply to function and to do the most ordinary things. And finding good help for a troubled individual is not something that most families face every day. How does one go about finding a counselor? Who should it be? How long will it take to make things better? What will it cost? When should it be done?

Only one of these questions has an easy answer: When should it be done? The answer is: immediately. Immediately, because tomorrow is a long way away for someone in pain. Immediately, because for some, desperate enough and hurting enough, tomorrow may never come.

As difficult as the problems seem, once that first step is taken, others seem to fall into place. Where does one find a counselor? Some experts in teen suicide suggest that a family who suspects a problem may begin by talking with the family doctor or pediatrician. That physician would undoubtedly be able to refer the family to a clinic or an individual with experience. Other resources that families can call upon may be the school guidance counselor, a crisis intervention center, or a local hospital. If money is an issue—and when is it not?—there are plenty of good clinics and clinicians who will see patients on a sliding scale basis (flexible fees adjusted to income). The point is to start somewhere. And to start immediately. One can always correct any problems later. But the crucial issue is to do something now. To provide enough caring that the individual can allow him/herself the *time* to feel better, the time to live, and eventually, the time to heal.

If it's a friend who is in trouble, this may be an even easier task, since young people are often more willing to talk with their peers than with adults. Since families can also be part of the problem (as Kelly said, "Families can be a *big* problem"), families cannot—sometimes—be seen as part of the solution. Also, some teens and young adults see older people as downplaying the problems of adolescence. Peers, facing similar problems, certainly do not downplay them. Finally, some studies show that suicidal teens are most likely to confide in close friends. It would seem, therefore, that peers have the best chance of reaching the one who is in crisis.

How, then, does one go about it?

One might begin with a simple statement such as "You seem kind of down lately." Followed, perhaps, by asking, "Is anything wrong?" This may be all it takes. Then, according to the experts, it is important to listen. To ask questions. And then to get help. Perhaps the most important single thing for anyone—young or old—to remember is never to allow oneself to be caught in a trap of secrecy. If a friend confides that he/she is contemplating suicide and wants to swear you to secrecy about the plans, it is imperative that you unveil that secret. Better a live angry friend than a dead one. And for the most part, the friend will not be angry. One who is talking about suicide is also—consciously or unconsciously—asking for help.

But what does one say to a friend who seems deeply distressed? Isn't it risky to even talk about it? Doesn't talking about suicide increase the risk that the individual will carry through with it?

How a friend reacts to another's cry for help may mean the difference between life and death, but experts say that it is not so much the exact words one chooses, but rather that one chooses to talk about it at all. Dr. Pamela Cantor, one of the country's leading experts on teen suicide, says that one will never give a young person the idea of killing him/herself just by talking about it. Just the opposite may be true. Knowing that someone cares and is available may be the very factor that saves a life.

There are, however, some general things to remember when talking to a friend or loved one who may be suicidal. The individual needs and deserves serious attention. Advice is not needed at this point. What *is* needed is for the sad or depressed friend to feel that someone else knows what he/she is feeling. It might even help for the listener to imagine what it's like to be in the other person's place.

Possibly equaling that in importance is that the listener display care and compassion, *without judgment*. No matter how trivial the person's problems may seem to you, it's important to remember that the problems are very real and even life-threatening to that individual. The listener who can convey that kind of nonjudgmental concern may very well be a lifesaver.

All threats to commit suicide, express or implied, ought to be taken seriously. Help should be sought. This is not the time to make your own judgment that the individual is or is not serious, is or is not just looking for attention. *All threats to commit suicide must be taken seriously.* If a friend is saying things that are scary, if the listener feels frightened, it's important to say so. And then to act on it.

Some innocent-sounding comments, intended to cheer up a sad friend, may well backfire. Statements such as "You don't know how well off you are" or "Look how much you have to live for" may only increase the feelings of guilt and worthlessness. After all, a sad and depressed person may think, if everyone else thinks I have everything to live for, what's wrong with me that I can't feel that way?

Similarly, statements meant to get the individual moving—"Cheer up! Snap out of it!"—while well-intentioned, may make the feelings worse. Here again, it's perhaps not a bad idea to put oneself in the place of the troubled individual. After all, each of us has felt sad and troubled at times. Imagine how we might have felt if, at the depths of our own sadness, someone had said, "Snap out of it!" Surely, we'd think, we would if we could.

But what does one say if, after asking a friend if he/she feels sad enough to be thinking of suicide, the friend replies yes?

For most of us, this is a scary thought. What to say? What to do? Did our question put the thought into the friend's mind? No. As stated before, talking about suicide will never put the idea of suicide into a person's head. Obviously, the individual has already been thinking about it. At this point, it's wise to ask if a plan has already been made. If the answer is yes, the crisis is imminent. The danger is immediate. Help should always be summoned if a friend is talking about or thinking of suicide, but if a plan has already been made, then the individual should not, if possible, be left alone. A parent, a teacher, a counselor—anyone with whom the troubled individual feels comfortable—should be summoned. Telling a friend that you care enough to get help may be necessary. If the friend becomes angry—so be it. No one—teen, young adult, or older adult—can handle a crisis such as this alone. No one, regardless of age or expertise, should be asked to take on this burden alone.

To repeat Kelly's words: "I don't believe that anyone who feels like committing suicide really wants to die. It's just a matter of not wanting to live life as it is right then, and not seeing another alternative. It's hard to see any other options. And kids see it as life *as it is.*"

It is up to us then, those in whom the sad or depressed person has confided, to help provide the time, the space, for the healing process to take place, so that life can change. So that it is no longer, life *as it is,* but life as it can become.

Chapter 4

Kelly O'Connor, Part 2

Getting through Tough Times
Coping after a Crisis
Teen Suicide Support Groups
The Importance of Talking and Listening

Kelly O'Connor had much more information to impart about severe depression and suicidal preoccupation. In the section to come, for example, she leaned forward in her chair and spoke with a certain intensity. "I wish I could say more to kids," she said. "You just never seem to find the right words. Maybe just this: If you choose to live now, you can choose to die later. But if you choose to die now, you can't choose to live later. It just doesn't work that way."

Kelly hit upon something frequently discussed by mental health experts: the apparent thought on the part of some teens that they *can* choose to die now—and then choose to live later.

Some experts who work with suicidal teens say that young people sometimes lack the maturity to recognize the *finality* of the act of suicide. These experts point out that this seems especially true of the "contagion" effect occasionally seen in youth suicide—that is, when one young person in a community chooses to die, and other young people then do likewise. According to these experts, a person contemplating suicide can have a kind of vague, unconscious thought that one will be able to reap the benefits of one's own death—one will somehow still be around to see what happens. The person may have the unconscious fantasy that he or she will be able to see how sad others are, how much he/she is missed, or how he/she may be viewed as tragic or important or both—perhaps when the individual did not feel important in life. In addition, say these experts, the person who is choosing suicide is sometimes trying to say, "I'll show them"—whoever "them" might be—for whatever "they" may have done. The problem here, of course, as the mental health experts point out, is that the dead person will never *know* how sad others are, how he/she is missed, or whether he/she has "gotten even."

But *do* teens really think this way? Doesn't such a statement do a disservice to young people—implying that they are too stupid to recognize that dead is *dead*? Research and study do seem to support the statement that *some* youths *sometimes* do not recognize the awful finality of death. Intellectually, yes; emotionally, no. Stupidity has nothing to do with it. The full reality of death, the full meaning of death is simply beyond comprehension for most of us—but especially beyond comprehension when one is young. As one teen in Chapter 7 says to her friends about the inevitability of death: "Do any of you *really* believe you're going to die?"

It is for this awareness of the finality of death, and the dawning recognition of what life could bring, that I complete the interview with Kelly O'Connor here. Even in her most depressed moments, Kelly recognized that if she chose suicide she would not be back to have a second chance, that she had to be stopped now.

A second reason for completing the interview with Kelly and her counselor, Dr. Skowronski, is equally important. Together, they point out that just because one gets through one tough time, there is no guarantee that there will never be another hard time. However, having another hard time doesn't necessarily mean that one will be suicidal or terribly depressed again. All it means is that life is a process—that it doesn't get all wrapped up in a neat little package. All lives have good times and all lives have some tough times. There is a background of strength to call upon for the one who has made it through the toughest of tough times—a recognition that: I made it once; I can make it again.

———

Questions were posed to Kelly about the kind of treatment she received when her distress signals were finally heard. How did it feel to know that she was finally going to get the help she sought? Was it a relief? Or was it frightening? She had originally gotten "help" that wasn't help. Did she finally get real help?

K: I was going to go in the hospital that day, the day that I finally told the school nurse how desperate I felt. But it didn't work out for that day and it was going to be the next day. I wasn't looking forward to having to spend the night at my house, after my parents really knew I had to go to the hospital. The next day, my best friend, Andrea, went with us up to the hospital, and my sister, Lisa, and my parents. The whole drive up there, I kept thinking: My problems can't be this bad. Let's turn around. I kept hoping the hospital would fade away from the face of the earth before we got there. Then we got lost, and I thought: Great! It did!

But of course, we did get there. We drove into the grounds. It was a really nerve-racking experience for me—the first time I had spent a significant amount of time away from home, other than spending a weekend at a friend's house. We went up to the young people's unit, and the staff got me settled in.

At that time I couldn't give them a commitment that I wasn't going to try something to hurt myself. They had to take away things like my razor and my hair dryer and lock them up in a room called "Sharps." They had me on what they called "eyesight"—meaning I had to be within eyesight of an assigned staff member at all times.

I was talking to Andrea, and then my family began getting ready to leave. They were leaving without me! I was in this strange place with all these people I didn't know. Andrea handed me something, and told me that she wanted me to think about her whenever I wore it. She left, and I looked at it. She'd given me her ID bracelet.

That's when I really fell apart.

All the other kids on the unit—they all came around and began helping me out and all, being really nice. I couldn't believe it. I just began crying in front of all these strangers. I mean, *I don't cry!* Remember, I only cry with my cat? It was a really strange experience. Because it felt good. It felt good in the sense that I felt safe.

Q: Instantly?

K: I could really feel that they cared. And knowing that I was on "eyesight," that they cared enough to be watching me so that I wouldn't do anything to myself . . .

This is hard to put into words. But I wouldn't trade that hospital experience for having never gone through the depression and all the pain. I learned so much about myself and about other people there. I met people who really changed my perspective on things. Here was this place full of people who cared about me. And who really understood. It was really a good feeling.

I was there for exactly three months, twenty-six days, and twenty hours. It was hard for me to leave when the time came, because the people had really gotten to be friends of mine.

When I left there, I still hated school and I was sure I would never go back. I'd find something else to do. But I did graduate from high school. I made it through my senior year by vowing never to go back.

But now I'm in college.

Q: Why?

K: Why? Because when I came out of the hospital, I wanted to be a psychiatric treatment worker. I discovered it's hard to find a job in that field without a degree. At first I decided I'd have to give up that goal. I went through a program called "Womanpower," training for nontraditional jobs. When I graduated from that program, I decided I wanted to go back to school. At that point, I was ready.

Q: How are you doing with school now?

K: It's another very rewarding experience for me. The people in the Human Services Department in my school are a lot like the people at the hospital. You can really tell that they care. They're a little bit crazy—and a lot of fun. First quarter I made Dean's List! And that felt good.

This quarter, I had some problems. My mother has cancer and had to have surgery. Even before that happened, some depression had started building up. I wasn't sure what it was coming from, but it started interfering with school-work. Work wasn't getting done again, and I was getting incompletes. I started seeing a psychologist in the school.

Now I'm in the process of getting the incompletes finished up—in fact, today I'm finishing up one of the papers.

Q: Have you had continuing care since your hospitalization—someone to talk to?

K: The group here, and I was seeing the doctor from the hospital. But I didn't go regularly for too long. I'd stop and then start again if I needed to.

Q: Do you think other kids would benefit from some continuing care after they've been through their crisis?

K: Definitely. At least to get the transition down. Because it's really hard. It was hard for me mostly because I had gotten so attached to the people.

———

Therapists who work with troubled youths point out that the period of transition from a protected, secure environment (such as the hospital that Kelly was in) back to the normal teen world is an important and sometimes difficult one. Much thought and cooperation between teens and their counselors and families may be necessary to make the transition successfully. It is a period that can't be rushed, and will require help and understanding. It may be useful to know that one will occasionally backslide. One won't necessarily feel suicidal or deeply depressed again. But one may feel sadness and fear and even some turmoil. It's important and encouraging to know that certain of these feelings are normal ones. That they will pass. And that one will be functioning on one's own again.

It is not only young people who have spent time in hospitals for whom this transition is necessary. Anyone who is moving from major supportive therapy to coping on one's own may expect to find this a difficult time. Some therapists compare it to a game that children play—one giant step forward, a few small steps (and occasionally a big one) backward. It's normal. It's a part of growth and adjustment to a new way of life, a new way of thinking.

Q: Kelly, you've mentioned how quickly you felt the caring from the people at the hospital—is that something you felt you were missing before that time?

K: Well, I knew that my family cared. I knew that they wanted to help. It's just that I—I think that I had so isolated myself from the family. I didn't feel that they could really understand. All the anger I had held in over the years made it very hard for me to really *care* that they cared. It didn't make that much difference. It made more of a difference that my friends cared. It was always easier to talk to them. And when I went in the hospital, I immediately felt very much attached to those people. Like they were really in tune to what I was feeling, and they really cared about me.

Q: What do you think friends can do for friends who feel so bad—maybe as bad as you did?

K: Friends let me know that they cared, and they cared enough to worry about me. And that helped a lot. And when it got to the point where I couldn't take it anymore, when I was going to do something, they cared enough to go ahead and tell someone about it.

Q: So if a friend is swearing another to secrecy, is saying, "I'm going to kill myself and don't tell anybody"—then you're saying they should tell?

K: There's no comparison—it's between losing a friendship and losing a life. Anyone who tells someone else that they're suicidal wants someone to stop them. A person who really gets to the point of choosing to die—that person is not going to tell anyone. People who get to that point can hide that very well.

But anyone who *tells* someone is still looking for another way. For a different way of dealing with it. For another chance at being happy. They're just *hoping* that someone else will do something to stop them. Because they don't have the energy to stop themselves.

Q: Does the depression take away your energy?

K: Yes. It's hard to say, "Okay, I need to start seeing a psychiatrist and put a lot of effort into working on these problems." You don't want to commit yourself to that. And end up maybe not doing it. It's a lot easier to get somebody to *make* you do it. To make you get help. That's the way it was with me. I couldn't say, "I *want* to go into a psychiatric hospital." I had to have someone say that I *needed* that, that I *had* to do that. And make it not a matter of my choice.

Q: Do you think other people feel that way?

K: Yes.

Q: Is there anything you could say to others who might feel suicidal—is there something you might suggest they could do?

K: The only thing is to know that there *is* another way. What a lot of teenagers may not realize is that if they try and get help and it doesn't work out, then the option to kill yourself is always there. But if they choose to die, then they can't choose to live later.

There are so many different types of treatment, so many different places besides a hospital. And different people. And it's not a matter of getting into a psychiatric hospital and then not being able to get out. I think a lot of people are afraid that once you're in, that's it—they lock the door behind you and you can't get out. But that's not really the case.

I wish I could say more to kids. You just never seem to find the right words. Maybe just this: If you choose to live now, you can choose to die later. But if you choose to die now, you can't choose to live later. It just doesn't work that way.

Dr. Skowronski: As Kelly's been talking about contemplating suicide and yet *wanting* to be stopped, I've been thinking of what other kids in the group and my other teenage groups say—that they fight against what they want. It's sort of "Please hear what I'm not saying."

Q: What do you mean?

Dr. S: Most people do want to be heard—do want help—but they don't know how to ask for it. At least, I know that almost everybody I've met wants help.

So, since they don't want to go to an adult for help—it's very rare that anyone in that age group will go to an adult—they go to their peers. And usually they'll ask their friends, "Please don't tell anyone."

Many teenagers say to me, "Oh, I don't want to break that confidence, because I'll break my friendship." Confidence and confidentiality is a very important issue with kids. But every peer can break that confidentiality. Because, as Kelly so succinctly said, better to break that friendship than to lose a friend forever.

Q: And as Kelly has also said, maybe it's not a confidence at all, but a cry for help?

Dr. S: Yes. They want you to *drag* them to a hospital. Or *drag* them to some kind of help.

Q: Because they don't have the energy to do it themselves?

Dr. S: The energy, the concentration level, is zip, nothing. That's why you can't do anything, can't do homework, can't concentrate. What's happening is you're unable to concentrate on anything because you're wasting your energy—you can't help it, the energy is being wasted for you. If you've ever been depressed, you know that's what happens. The energy is gone. Then you get more angry at yourself because you can't do anything. And then anger gets turned inward.

So teens go to someone their age because they know it'll be someone who will understand them. Understanding is the key word. And an adult sometimes has a great deal of trouble understanding a teenager. We want to forget how we felt when we were going through that period. We don't want to recall the pain. As Kelly said, there are bills to be paid, other things to do, and so adults' lives get complicated with other things. We tend to forget those very awkward, *difficult* years that we all went through. And we all had feelings of suicide, by the way. Maybe we didn't do anything about them, but we've all had feelings that "maybe the world would be better off without me." And that's particularly true if you're a sensitive person. So, once the teen years are over, we adults want to forget.

Q: Could the parents' denial also be because it hurts so much for parents to see their kids hurting?

Dr. S: Exactly. So parents sometimes say, "Oh, well, they'll work through it. *I* worked through it. Pull up the old bootstraps and just get on with it." Which is *not* what a teenager needs to hear.

That's also why statements such as—"Oh, you're wonderful, oh, you're great. Hey, all you have to do is just get through this little period and everything's going to be fine"— that kind of thing just makes a person who's depressed go up the wall. Because it doesn't help a bit.

And saying things like "Look at your wonderful family—you have four brothers, mother, father—"

K: Words like that tell you that the person doesn't understand!

Dr. S: Yes. And it also makes you feel guiltier. Because you already *know* that you have these people who love you and care for you.

K: For me, once I decided definitely to do it, I was ecstatic about it. My problems were going to be over. But immediately something else was going "Uh-oh. Wait a minute. There's something big-time wrong to be this happy about killing yourself." It was like two opposing forces. Then people say, "Think of your family, think of what it would do to them." And you're thinking: Think of what it's doing to *me!* Now! You really feel misunderstood.

Dr. S: That's one of the things I had to more or less demythologize myself about. Because I always thought a person who was suicidal, *really* making plans, *really* going to do something about it, was someone who was *not* surrounded by loving family or friends. When in truth many are. As we find in the group.

Q: Could you tell me a little about the group? How it works—and how it might work for others?

Dr. S: The group is run by a number of different counselors besides me—three of us who are trained. Last night, for instance, we had seventy kids in the group. We were talking about feelings, feelings that we have all gone through about being lonely. The theme was "Alone in the Crowd." All the kids were really involved in communicating with each other. It was so exciting to hear them able to speak about their deepest emotion. Because it's hard—how *do* you tell your deepest emotion if you're really hurting?

Kelly is able to speak it now because in a way she's rehearsed it by talking to doctors, peers, and others. Most people do it in silence. And that silence is detrimental.

Kelly has just recently come back, and she's such a welcome addition to the group—almost as a role model. She can eloquently express how she feels about what she's gone through. She can point out that it's not as though once you've been through depression, you'll *never have it again.* But it also doesn't mean that you're *suicidal* again. It just means: I made it once, I can make it now again. It's very

37

important for a person who is suicidal to hear that. Kelly knows how they feel.

We were trying to decide on names for this group. I was caught up in all that "initial" stuff—making up initials to stand for a name. But at our first meeting the kids said, call it what it is—Suicide Prevention. But it does take time for parents to agree to this.

Sometimes we have trouble getting kids to this group. We have to rely on parents to drop their kids off (if the kids aren't driving yet). And a great number of parents don't agree that they have any problems in the family.

Kelly used to pick kids up and bring them here. Frankly, we need that. Kids will call here, leave their number. When I call back, parents answer and say, "What do you want?" I say, "I'd like to speak to Chris"—or whoever left the message. And the parent says, "Well, she's fine."

It's very difficult to get parents to agree that there's any problem. Sometimes they agree only when their child does what Kelly did.

Q: Do you think parents today are just not hearing?

Dr. S: Well, our parents didn't hear us, either. I mean, I love my mother, but there were some things we didn't talk about, either. No, it's not just parents today. It was true of our parents, too. It's very hard to communicate with parents. It's just not something you normally do at certain ages. In the first place, you wouldn't *want* your mother and father to know everything about you. Even to this day, there are certain things I wouldn't tell my mother.

But the defense mechanisms are up with families if they have to take their kids to a support group.

Q: So it's not just today? There have been similar problems all along?

Dr. S: No, there are some things different. It's coping mechanisms that it seems to me are missing today. What we're trying to do with our suicide prevention council, all the agencies that are trying to help with teens—the Y, the child abuse agencies, the councils on crime—is get a curriculum written and get it in the schools. We've just persuaded the superintendent of schools that it is needed—some kind of program that will help a person learn how to cope.

You know, all the time that Kelly sat in front of the TV alone, eating her dinner, spending seven hours a night on homework, is not healthy. What could have changed that? She had some problems at home. Well, we've had problems at home with parents forever, and always will. So why did it affect Kelly? Why has it affected others her age more than it did ten years ago? We don't know. But maybe if there had been a program in schools that dealt with feelings, that said, "How do you feel when a parent does or says what your parent said or did?"—it might have helped Kelly find different ways of coping.

That's what we're seeing—that if we deal with the problems as they come up, it is helpful. That's why the suicide support group is so helpful. Why talking to a psychiatrist is helpful. Talking to someone who understands.

It comes out often in the support group: that it is all right to talk about suicidal feelings. It is okay to say it. It is okay to share it. That doesn't mean you're going to do it. It doesn't mean you're crazy or sick. It just means you're hurting.

Therapy is a process, just as it was a *process* getting to the point of being suicidal. Suicide is not just one impulsive act. By seventeen years old, a person has usually given it some thought—some great thought. Usually most of us don't speak about what's deep inside us. But when we use silence, we close down. What we try to do with the group is help them talk about—and hear about—some of the feelings *all* of us have been through. That's what this group is all about—suicide *prevention*.

———

Dr. Skowronski did not suggest talking as a panacea, a quick cure for the depression and sadness afflicting young people today. But watching and listening to Kelly, hearing in her own words the story of her change from one who was silent and depressed and suicidal to one who is verbal and happy and involved in life again, one could not help thinking that talking—talking with peers, friends, professionals, parents—and listening—does make a difference.

Is it scary—or risky—to talk about such things? Dr. Skowronski makes an important point: that it *is* all right to talk about one's feelings—even about one's suicidal feelings. It *is* all right to think it. But it's *not* all right to do it.

Another point bears repeating—that just as getting to the point of despair was a "process," possibly made up of many small and large incidents, so working through those feelings is a process. It can be very helpful for a depressed individual to recognize that, to know that one doesn't suddenly become better, that one's depression doesn't suddenly lift. Believing that it does get better suddenly or quickly might make an individual even more depressed. "Why am I *still* not happy?" a young person might question. Much of life is a process, and sometimes working through certain feelings is a *slow* process.

Yet that process need not be a totally sad or painful one. Rather, it can be a positive process, a joyful one—as Kelly said, a "really good feeling."

Chapter 5

Richard Klein

Advice from a Suicide Survivor
From a Male's Point of View
Rock Music Lyrics
Substance Abuse
Causes of Depression
Suicide Hotlines

R̶ichard Klein is confined to a wheelchair because of injuries caused by his failed suicide attempt while he was in high school.

When I first heard of Rich Klein, he was active as a speaker in high school suicide prevention programs, talking in part about the pressures on young people today. Rich could speak about these pressures because they had almost overwhelmed him at one time. I was very much interested in learning more about just this subject.

I began by reading articles about Rich and looking at pictures of him—an extremely handsome young man in his twenties, a former baseball star now confined to a wheelchair.

I called Rich and asked if he would meet with me. We met in his room in his apartment in Los Angeles, California.

The room is specially equipped with hospital bed, railings, mirrors, and many of the other things that make it convenient for an occupant who lives all of his days in a wheelchair. He was not only willing to talk about his suicide attempt—and what he's learned since—but also eager. I later learned that Rich talks to whomever he can meet—high school students, college students, older people. His concern is to talk about living and ultimately to coerce people into deciding that life, for all the hard times, is worth living.

Rich's conclusions blew away some of my own preconceptions. He is only one person, but I think he speaks for a lot of teens when he talks about the pressures that young people experience today. Since he is a man, he talks, obviously, about some pressures that only young men feel. On other issues, his thoughts may have broader validity.

An interesting aspect of this interview was Rich's similarity in some ways to Kelly. When he spoke of his pain in personal relationships, and his withdrawal and inability to speak of it, he could almost have been speaking in Kelly's voice. No one knew, in either of their lives, that they were literally dying of pain.

There was one other striking similarity. Both Rich and Kelly spoke, not only of their silence, but also of their acting ability, their considerable ability to hide from anyone the pain that was going on inside. "Me? Tip off anyone as to how I was feeling?" says Rich. "Of course not. I put on a good show in public."

And Kelly, using different words, says the same thing. "I'd come in, the smile would go on—'nothing's wrong, everything's fine.' I was always very good at acting."

There were certain similarities in their behavior, but there were many, many differences. Rich speaks of how social and national events influenced him. Media, news events, music had such a profound effect on him that he believes they played a part in his decision about whether he would live or die.

For Kelly, although her pain and depression were similar to Rich's, the world and society in general seemed to play little role in her depression and did not affect at all her decision about whether or not to go on living.

This was an interesting contrast for me to see—and one that I continued to see throughout my interviews—that although some young people showed similar traits, particularly silence and withdrawal and the ability to hide their pain, still, for the most part, each person's pain is unique.

Rich began by talking about his feelings just prior to his suicide attempt.

R: Depression. I felt so depressed. And lonely. I was scared—like a mouse living in a stray-cat alley. I wanted out.

Yet I never cried. I wanted to, but actually couldn't. My stomach felt so twisted and icy I could barely eat. I would sleep for two hours a night, with luck. I felt I had to get out. And out meant suicide.

Q: What brought on those feelings?

R: I felt I had some major things coming down on me. Major personal problems—loneliness, the need to hide my feelings. Hey, I was this big baseball player—but I hid the fact that I wrote songs and poetry. There were other things that even today I can't talk about completely—not with everyone, anyway. All very personal feelings. Personal relationships were always a problem for me. Also, not expressing myself was a problem. I had feelings that I should have talked about and I didn't. I think now that I made

them out to be a lot more than they were. I don't know—
I'm still trying to put some things in perspective. But back
then, I just felt that things were haunting, threatening,
closing in on me from all directions. I was so lonely. So
alone.

Q: Did you have anyone to talk to?

R: Me? Tip off anyone as to how I was feeling? No,
of course not! I had some good friends and a great family,
but it was *my* business to take care of everything myself.
At six foot two and two hundred pounds, could Big Rich
admit to anyone, even himself, that he was going under?
After all, I wasn't nuts! I could still put on a good show in
public. In conversation with friends and family, I went
through the superficial stuff. And there was a solution.
Suicide. I didn't know what else to do.

It was a beautiful morning, March 26. I drove to a
huge dam a few miles from home. No one had survived a
fall from it. It's about ninety to a hundred feet high on the
dry side, where the cement and gullies are.

I was standing on the side of the steps that go way up.
Another man was there—a stranger. I learned later who he
was—Mark Allen, a medical student. He looked at me. He
was feeling depressed that day, too, he said later. And when
he looked at me, he wanted to talk to me. But he didn't.
He went down the steps. I went up. He was sitting, just
like you are. He said he heard this noise. He turned around,
and he saw me go off.

I didn't jump. I just rolled off the top as if I were tossing
around in bed. The last thing I remember saying was "God,
forgive me."

Mark saw me hit once, hit twice, and then hit again
another eighty feet down. I was always conscious, though
I didn't know what was what. They tell me I was giving
my phone number and address and answering questions.

But I don't remember anything till three weeks later. I didn't know what was going on. I didn't care who was dead around me, just so long as I was dead. Paralyzed makes you want to be dead anyway.

But that day, when I did it, Mark ran off and got help, and they had a rescue team. I was up in the crevice in the rocks. I'm the only one, in seventy years, who survived a fall from that dam. And I thank that rescue team. And I love Mark very much, believe me.

Q: You're glad, then, that they rescued you.

R: Are you kidding? Very much. Very, very much.

Q: So that no matter how bad it feels today, tomorrow may be different?

R: Right. I tell kids, don't judge everything by the present.

Q: Rich, to look at you, and to read of your accomplishments, at least to the outside world, you seemed to have had everything going for you—

R: *Seemed to* . . . because I always wanted to play the John Wayne macho role, which is baloney now as far as I'm concerned. What does macho mean? That you're not supposed to express your feelings? Men have loads of feelings, conflicting feelings. But we play the role. Put on a front. I never talked to many people about anything. Writing songs was a great outlet for me. But it was *my* world. I never felt I wanted to expose my feelings to other people. I still don't, but I was *really* bottled up at that time.

Q: Do you think it would have helped if you had talked some?

R: I think I should have sought out *more* people. You know, there's certain things you can tell your parents, and there's certain things you can tell your friends. But I built a wall a thousand times around myself. Because I was too "cool" to talk to anyone. The John Wayne baloney. Look, we see it on TV: "Don't cry, kid!" Guys have it tough.

Q: Is it harder then, do you think, for men? Because they feel they have to protect an image?

R: Yeah. I played baseball. I was in the business of delivering appliances. But you know, I *snuck off* to meetings of the Song Writer's Guild? Not many people knew it at all. It was my own private world.

Q: What other things were problems for you besides that need to protect an image—things that might relate to young people today?

R: Negativism. Fear. Both of the present and the unknown. Fear of the unknown was a great one. Personal relationships, as I said before. And not expressing myself. Feelings that I should have talked about but didn't. See, I care what people think. But I won't let that govern what I do. Not anymore.

Q: Is that concern for what others think—peer pressure—a big factor in young people's lives today, too?

R: Kids love to point the finger at each other. No matter what happens, if they're in their little group, they'll point it. Kids say, "Oh, wow, you did this? You did that?" It could be masturbating, drinking, smoking, or else someone says, "Hey, you faggot." Kids of fifteen or so have all kinds of sexual feelings. People have lots of sexual feelings all through their lives. Those things are nothing to be ashamed of. It's human nature.

Sex creates a lot of tension for kids. It always did for me when I was younger. I didn't know a lot about it. Some things about it literally shouldn't be picked up on the streets.

Q: Do you think that has an effect on young people—their natural insecurities about their own sexualities?

R: I think sex is judged as a performance. When I played baseball, the guys would say, "Hey, I did this or that last night. What did you do?" Who cares, man? Does that prove one's masculinity? Not for me it doesn't. Never did. What does it mean if you're not communicating love, physically and verbally? You're just going through the motions.

Q: Before, you mentioned the aloneness.

R: Oh, yeah. Aloneness. You know, songs I wrote way back then are so prophetic—about what I eventually did.

Q: So this wasn't just one impulsive act?

R: I was always fascinated with death, with what death was or wasn't. In fact, it was when John Lennon was murdered that I started writing songs. That death used to haunt me. Constantly. I remember it was on "Monday Night Football," Miami was playing New England, and Howard Cosell announced that John Lennon was murdered. I thought about that for two years afterward. Not so much that he died, but the way he died. At one of the best points of his life. He got out of his car, Mark David Chapman said, "Mr. Lennon?" and boom, boom, boom, boom. That was it. And then plane crashes, like Buddy Holly. Also Elvis Presley. And the way *he* died—incredibly sad.

Q: What does the way these individuals died mean to you?

R: It's just the connotation of death, and how society almost glorifies it. Society makes you out to be a super guy when you're not there to speak about it. But that's not really why *I* did it. I didn't really care what people thought at the time. It was just me, me and my own mind that created disaster.

Q: But you were influenced, at least in your thoughts, by these others who had so much going for them and yet died?

R: It just fascinates me, what death is. But now I don't want to get there. Not yet. You know, I think we see death as a way to ease the pain. I think we see it sometimes as a *temporary* solution. We see it every day on television—and we think, oh, he got shot, well, he'll be back next day. And even the songs on the radio. There's one of them that starts off, "Sometimes you're better off dead, there's a gun in your hand and it's pointed at your head." Very detrimental lyrics.

Q: Do you think young people hearing those lyrics are influenced by them?

R: I think rock is one of the greatest influences around. It always was for me. It still is.

———

Whatever one's bias, the issue of rock music and its influence on young people obviously calls up very strong emotions. Much has been said and written about it in the media and elsewhere, but few solid conclusions have been drawn. It is true, however, that others have expressed feelings similar to Rich's. There are those who argue that such a position is improbable, that no one—teen or adult—could be influenced to behave in a certain way because of a particular song. How, they argue, could one say for sure that *this* particular song caused *this* particular act of violence against oneself?

Obviously, much more research needs to be done before a fair assessment of such statements can be made. (In Chapter 7 of this book, one group of teens discuss this. Some believe as Rich does, and others believe the very opposite.)

For now, if any conclusion might be drawn from Rich's experience, perhaps it should be only that he believes such music influenced *him*.

———

Q: Do you think lyrics that glorify death helped you to see death as an answer?

R: I must have subconsciously thought a lot about that. A lot of my own songs deal with that. There was a quote once by someone who said something like "It's better to burn out than fade away." What does that mean? It's a horrible thing to say. How many ways can you burn out? By drugs, alcohol? By what I did? Some of these guys are out there making money so they say whatever they want to say. That's not the example *I* want to set. I tell kids right now that what I did is horrible.

Q: Had you had any help before your suicide attempt? Anyone to talk to?

R: No. I was always moody. Many times I'd just sort of close up. But now I talk a lot more. I don't talk about everything. I don't think anyone has to get completely inside a kid's head—I'm not going to ask anyone the intricacies of his or her personality. But anything anyone tells me isn't going to shock me, either. Because I've probably done most of it anyway. Except drugs. I don't know much about drugs. I always think that you and your mind are the best and worst drug. You can create disaster or greatness with your mind.

Q: Do you think that drugs are a form of suicide, too?

R: I think drugs are a form of long-term suicide. It may start out as just for kicks, or as a way to ease the pain. But you can get hooked.

According to a report by the American Association of Suicidology, nearly half of the youths who had died by suicide in that particular study were involved in alcohol or drug abuse shortly before their deaths.

Another report by Dr. David Brent, a psychiatrist at the University of Pittsburgh working with the coroner for Allegheny County, found similar statistics. According to his study, the proportion of young people who killed themselves while intoxicated rose to 46% by 1983—more than three times the rate of ten years earlier. (No statistics were available on the presence of drugs in the individuals.)

Other researchers point out that drugs and alcohol sometimes act as de-inhibitors, allowing individuals to act out their depressions and frustrations by suicide, when they might have acted differently had they not been under the influence of drugs.

This does not mean, however, that such substance abuse necessarily caused the deaths. Rather, it is probable that the things that led young people to try such substances—unhappiness, depressions, feelings of hopelessness—are the same things that led to their deaths by suicide.

In spite of the above reports, there are varying estimates among professionals about the actual percentage of involvement in drugs and alcohol among those who have died by suicide. Probably the most important fact to remember is that drugs, alcohol, and depression can be a lethal combination.

Q: What's different now—different in the way you see things, perhaps?

R: One of the things I've learned is that the less I know, the more I know—that's what I live by.

What's also different is this: Now there's guilt. Guilt still hurts. I can never forgive myself for what I did, even though good things are happening. Now I have my own cable TV show. I'm talking in the schools. I'm writing my own book, and also writing an exercise book for people in wheelchairs. Writing songs for a band—still doing that. A lot of good things are happening. But I can never forget every morning that I'm in this wheelchair. And every time I go by that dam, I remember.

Q: Go by the dam? You drive your own car?

R: Not yet. I'll be relearning—with hand controls. Guilt is a great motivator for me. It makes me work out harder. To become as independent as possible. And I am. I can transfer myself back and forth from my chair, dress myself, and do a lot of things—things that nobody thought I could.

I wrote a poem about guilt. Since this happened, I've written a lot of great stuff. Well, *I* think it's good stuff. Are you familiar with the song "Sunday Morning Coming Down"? For me, it was always *Monday* morning coming down— when I would come home from the rehabilitation center for a Sunday, and then would have to go back on Monday. I was in the hospital for about five months, and then at the rehab center about seven.

I'll recite the poem for you about guilt, okay? It's called "Gil's Eating Habits"—"Gil" for guilt.

The pain of Monday morning
Often gives me no warning.
It twists and gnaws savagely.
I'm half alive, struggling
In Gil, the panther's, jowls.
After a while I escape or am spat out.
Temporary freedom. I clean my wounds
Wear my invisible bandages
And roll through the day.
Sometimes, the panther is my friend.
He struts with me as I roll

And we are very strong together.
You know, his appetite ain't what it used to be.
He's losing weight and has a lot more discipline.
He really helps me work hard
When his stomach is kept in check,
But, like any beast, he gets hungry
And when the pickings are scarce
I'm always there for Gil to chew and eat.
Yes, I do want him here,
But someday, I hope he becomes a strict vegetarian.

I want him there to remember. You can use guilt as a motivator, or you can let it eat you.

I talk a lot more with my father and others now. And internally, I talk a lot with God—whoever or whatever the force of God is. I believe you have to put your faith somewhere. Kids can put their faith in God. Put their faith in a rock out there.

Q: But believe in something?

R: Yeah. Everyone and everything is put here for a reason. Even a grain of sand in the desert is here for a reason.

Q: Any more differences in yourself that you've noticed?

R: I'm willing to take help from others now. I learned that the hard way. I'm paralyzed from the chest down—it looks like from the waist down because I can bend over and do things and transfer myself back and forth. But I was *taught* by others how to do that, at the rehab center.

Q: Did you have other help—psychological help, afterward?

R: Yes, at the hospital. After a while, the therapist said—it seems all right; let me know if something comes up. And I will.

But now, a lot of my therapy comes from talking to kids. I've never had more of a purpose than I have now. Everything I've always wanted to do, I'm doing now—writing, doing the television show. But I'm not walking. Still, I never feel sorry for myself now. Never. I hope no one does. But I feel sorry for the man I was, who let himself get that far.

Another change in me is that I have a faith in God. I don't know who or what God is, but there is a force there. To have me land ninety feet down and just break my left wrist, right ankle, and my neck—and never lose any blood. And land next to a medical student. Well, I don't know. The less I know, the more I know.

What changed me? I'm not sure exactly—but I finally accepted that I am here for a reason. I really believe that. People live and die for reasons. I'm taking the initiative now. I'm in a wheelchair, I'm paralyzed physically. But I look at society and I see a lot of *mental* paralysis out there. Bigotry, for example. It's one of the worst paralyses there is. Bigotry hurts kids. Life is very precious. If I don't take the initiative, and try to do what I'm trying to do now, then I think I'd be wasting my second chance. I really do.

———

Rich has been focusing on one major reality to which others might relate—the reality of the pressures that he felt.

Rich's attempt on his life was extraordinary, but the pressures he felt to be "macho," to be secretive about his soft side, were pressures with which many young men might identify.

Men are not the only ones who cope with pressure and stress. The need to hide one's emotional side is but one of many pressures experienced by both men and women today. All young people spoke of coping with a variety of stresses, some more intense than others. Perhaps the one I heard most often was the need to live up to standards— standards that are not necessarily one's own. Many young people feel they must do what their parents, teachers, peers expect of them, sometimes when those expectations are in direct conflict with their own.

Several common examples that teens mentioned frequently: finding themselves forced into careers they didn't choose, colleges they didn't want to attend, even forms of recreation in which they didn't want to participate—all because of the expectations of others. It's not parents who place these pressures and expectations on young people. Sometimes it is peer pressure—as is seen often in the area of sexual matters.

This is not new, nor is it necessarily a cause of severe depression on the part of young people today. But if an individual is coerced into actions or behaviors with no chance to say, "Hey, this is not right for me!", it can sometimes begin a downward spiral of negative and hopeless feelings about one's life in general.

In addition to such personal pressures, there has been much speculation about other kinds of pressures: the specter of nuclear war that hangs over their futures. The AIDS epidemic. The sense of rootlessness that comes from the breakup of homes. The ease and availability of drugs. All of these can have a depressing effect on young people today. And while probably not one of them is a single cause of the increase in youth suicide, if an individual is already feeling depressed or sad, knowledge of such events can sometimes make the world seem a very bleak place.

Q: Rich, could you suggest ways for other people to *not* be as alone and desperate as you were? Should they confide in someone—a friend, someone?

R: I think kids have to confide. But not necessarily in each other if they're afraid of rejection or whatever. But someone. I tell them to realize you're not alone. Realize that there are others. That you *seek out* others. And that there's suicide prevention. *I* looked it up in the phone book, but I think I was too far gone when I saw it.

———

Rich's community and certain other communities are fortunate to have a Suicide Hotline listed in the phone book, or something called a Crisis Hotline. Unfortunately, many other localities do not have this. If you need help, almost any agency listed in the *Yellow Pages* under "Social Services" will be able to refer you to someone who can help. Your local hospitals can also do the same. When someone answers, if you feel that you are in crisis and need help *immediately,* say so. Someone will be able to talk with you immediately. If that agency can't provide someone, call another, or have them call someone for you or refer you to a place that can help. It is not as hard as it sounds. Someone will respond if you tell them you are in crisis.

In addition, the Youth Suicide National Center in California is staffed twenty-four hours a day to respond to anyone needing *information.* (As an emergency hotline, they serve only areas in California.) They can suggest where you can go in your community for local help. That number is (415) 877-5604.

Finally, if your crisis is immediate, and you cannot wait to look up a number or dial any of the above numbers, simply dial 0 for Operator or, in some areas, 911 for emergencies. Tell anyone who answers that you are in a crisis and thinking of suicide and need someone to talk to immediately. Then stay on the line. Don't hang up. Someone will find a number for you or perhaps even make the connection for you to available help.

R: If I had looked up suicide prevention earlier, I would have realized I wasn't alone. Realized that there were other people. You know, I wrote a poem yesterday called "The Mask." We put on masks to be accepted, not rejected. To be liked, not disliked. To be loved, not hated. I think we all wear a mask before the world.

Q: And that mask is a barrier?

R: Yes. But I tell kids, take off that mask and realize you're not alone.

Q: But that's hard to do, isn't it? Is there something kids might do, something you'd suggest?

R: Yes. *Don't give up.* If I were talking to a kid right now, this is what I'd say: Be aware that others share in your suffering. That life is up and down and it's a struggle. But don't forget, it's also great. Don't forget the good things in life. Don't ever say, "Life stinks." *Situations* in life stink. If you ever think of suicide, I advocate running away. I'll advocate teenage runaways before I will suicide. Go away, start a new life. It's better than dying. I don't care where you go or what you do—you're still alive. You'll have time to reevaluate, meet other people, and learn some things. You can always take off, and always find others who will share. Go toward the place of your dreams. I don't care where it is.

Q: But do something—rather than die?

R: Anyone can die. It's no great feat. Oh, they'll think about it for a while: "Wow, he died, he went off the dam."

I don't want to be remembered for how I died. I want to be remembered for how I lived and for what I'm trying to do. Anybody can die. People *will* get over it eventually. But you just leave such a void. It's selfish, horribly selfish.

Q: So you think they *can* do something?

R: *I* could have. I *should* have. I could have confided in someone. For young people—go to a suicide prevention center, any mental health agency. Your problems are not any different than a lot of other people's. I know it feels so alone, but you're *not* alone.

Q: If you could say one final thing to young people, what might it be?

R: Pursue your dreams every day. It's the title of a song I wrote long ago. Can I recite it for you?

Follow me, let me show you something new.
Leave it all, it's not worth keeping anyway.
Start anew, you'll feel a certain kind of freshness.
Just be yourself, pursue your dreams every day.
Why should you copy everybody else?
Who's to say you must always fit the pattern?
Your ideas cast a light into the darkness.
Don't be afraid, pursue your dreams every day.
They will laugh and always whisper.
Never mind, they'll never prosper anyway.
Perhaps they'll have more money,
But will wake up hating every single day.
Because the clothes they wear
Are cut to fit the patterns they adhere to all the way.
So make your move.
Put the life back in your living.
Loneliness relates to knowing more than others.
Pace yourself, but don't you ever give up trying.
Success will come.
Pursue your dreams every day.

That's what I say. Go after it and share it more with others. Go after your dreams and live. Because anybody can die.

———————

Before talking with Rich, I wondered whether those who had made the most lethal attempts on their lives, having been saved once, would still want to die. Certainly Rich, with his serious attempt and his vigorous rehabilitation of himself afterward, seemed to say that for him at least, life is very precious. Obviously, broad conclusions cannot be drawn from just one individual. Yet therapists and researchers alike, as well as the individuals themselves, seem to be in agreement that most people are glad—joyous—to have a second chance. That no matter how bad things were—and for Rich, no matter how awful they were to become, with paralysis and loss of certain freedoms—life was even more worth living than before.

Reading this interview, some may say that Rich was a very foolish young person. And Rich may be the first to agree. However, in spite of his human feelings, his despair and feelings of self-destruction, Rich came back. With courage and determination, he came back to say to others: I was there. I know. I came back from that place. And you can, too.

Another point that Rich made repeatedly was the need to confide in someone, to talk about his problems. Yet he felt, and rightly so, that some things were private. He would not discuss—with me—his precise reasons for making an attempt on his life, although he disclosed that he was under pressure with many personal problems, including isolation and silence. However, Rich *was* talking to someone. The most personal "whys" of his suicide attempt were being worked out with a doctor at his hospital. Which is as it should be. He needed, as all of us need, to speak of the deepest pain—with *someone*. As Dr. Skowronski said in Chapter 4, "Usually most of us don't speak about what's deep inside us. But when we use silence, we close down. What we try to do . . . is *talk* about—and hear about—some of the feelings all of us have been through. That's what this is all about—suicide *prevention*." Another way of saying, perhaps, what Rich has been saying: that talking, talking to someone who really *hears,* is what suicide prevention is all about.

Finally, in considering this, the reader may wonder if there are not alternative ways to cope with one's troubles and fears. Yes, communication is always vital. Are there other ways of expressing, and perhaps of working out, the pain that each of us feels at times?

Many young people have found other creative ways of helping themselves through a difficult period in their lives. Some become physically active, taking an intense interest in and making a commitment to sports. Others find solace and creative outlet in writing. Still others find expression and release in theater, in music, in art. The method that one chooses doesn't matter. What matters only is that the person does something positive—takes that pain and does something with it, makes something useful out of it. Perhaps even something beautiful.

Such an alternative is explored in the following chapter.

Chapter 6

Heather Falk

Family Patterns of Suicide
Finding the Skills to Cope
Sharing the Burdens
The Importance of Creative Self-Expression

Heather Falk is a talented teenage artist who sought me out when she heard about the research I was doing for this project. Events in Heather's family background made her feel that she had important experience to contribute: Heather's sister had made a number of serious, suicidal attempts on her life, the first when Heather was about eight years old. Heather's mother had had suicidal tendencies, and her aunt had died from a self-administered overdose of medication.

Heather felt as though she, too, were somehow a victim. In addition, there was a kind of pact of secrecy and silence surrounding those suicides and suicide attempts. Heather now wanted to talk with others who had to deal with similar family secrets or burdens, to let them know that they were not alone.

Perhaps the most important aspect of Heather's interview is her point of view. Being less personally involved in (although not totally free from) feelings of suicidal despair and depressions than either Kelly or Rich—or her sister or mother or aunt—she is able to see events from a different perspective. Accordingly, she is able to speak about the stresses present in such a family, and how one can go about finding the necessary coping skills.

Occasionally, therapists say, one does encounter family patterns of suicide like this, and there is conflicting opinion about the causes. Some researchers feel that when an individual in a family kills him/herself, it puts the others more at risk—not because there is a known genetic link to suicide, but because this is thought to be learned behavior. In other words, if one individual takes his/her own life, it almost comes to seem an "acceptable option" for others to do the same.

Another group of researchers has found that there seems to be a link between low levels of a factor called serotonin in the blood, and a high incidence of suicides, suggesting that this biochemical imbalance may cause certain depressions.

Still other researchers are looking at other clues. Perhaps the only thing that can be said for certain today is that whatever cause may one day be discovered, family members of suicide victims are themselves somewhat more at risk of suicide than those who have never experienced a suicide within the family. However, researchers and therapists are quick to point out that suicide is an individual decision; that because a certain family member kills him/herself, it is not *inevitable* that others will follow.

In the following interview, Heather speaks first in general terms about her family history and then about her feelings as a sibling in that family. Then, more specifically, she suggests how kids today might cope with a similar situation. Finally, she talks about the role her art played in her life—how it helped her cope as a child, as well as what it means to her today. She then goes on to elaborate about how this and other forms of self-expression might liberate others.

———— ◆ ————

Heather: As a child, I felt like a victim of this incredibly volatile, emotional situation in my family.

It's just a kind of family history. My grandmother—she was a very dramatic person, always crying. I remember her always with her hand to her forehead. Everything was just too much for her. My mother's sister had killed herself. And, as I understand it, my mother also had suicidal tendencies.

And then my sister. I was about eight; she was fifteen. There were two suicidal instances that I recall with her—the first was when she attempted to attack herself with a knife, in front of me and my mother. The other time was an overdose of pills.

The night she overdosed, I was in bed and I heard all these sounds. I got up. She had taken sleeping pills, and we had to take her to the hospital. In the car on the way to the hospital, she was hallucinating. But during all this, I was never hysterical. I guess when you're around hysterical people, you tend to be just the other way. I would just be there—with big eyes. We got to the hospital and they had to care for her, and I was scooting around in a wheelchair. I remember just playing in that wheelchair.

But the guilt. I just always felt responsible in some way.

Q: For your sister?

H: For everyone. That was my role. You know how we get "assigned" roles in a family? Well, my role was good-natured. The good person in the family.

In addition, growing up in that volatile situation, I really learned to keep things away from me so that I could carry on—go to school and all.

Like the night my sister took the pills, I remember I didn't go to school next day because I'd been up so late. When I went back, it was sort of a "what if they knew?" situation. You know how your friends ask where were you? Well, I lied.

Q: You never were able to say why?

H: No. Never.

Q: Did your mother ever talk about it?

H: No! She never said a word. No one ever talked to me about it. Ever.

Q: Would it have helped if they had?

H: Yes. I know it would have been a tremendous help to have kids my own age, say, to talk to.

Q: Even as young as you were—eight or nine?

H: Oh, yes. Because children understand so much.

Q: So even though no one ever said, "Don't talk about what your sister did," still you got the message anyway, that this was something you shouldn't speak about?

H: That's right. And I still do get emotional talking about it. But I was always a very private person—not quiet; in fact, kind of loud and a leader of the pack. But very private. I never told anyone that I had all this stuff going on.

Q: Did you ever have a therapist when you were small?

H: My mother sent me to this psychiatrist when I was about nine. But this guy was asking me all these leading questions, and I remember lying to him. I remember thinking: he's not going to get to me. He'd ask me questions I knew were leading questions—like about my father. I'd say, "Oh, yes, I love to go fishing with my daddy." When I didn't. And he said to my mother that there was nothing to worry about.

Q: But you felt there was?

H: Yes. Because later on, when I was about thirteen and I went away to boarding school, I found myself being somewhat self-destructive. From being in this family.

I think it was learned behavior—adopting this dramatic "I just can't cope" attitude. I remember once—I didn't really want to kill myself—but I remember sitting high up in a loft in a barn, and agonizing over whether or not to leap off.

I remember being there for a long period of time. Picturing hurling myself down, and how it would feel. I was really consumed with that moment. It's as if you're daring yourself—can I get myself to do this? It seemed to be a moment of drawing things to a conclusion. Like it would be simple if this was it. I mean, if your whole life depends on what happens at that moment—then all those other things that you don't want to think about go away. So I guess, actually, it could have been flight as well.

The seduction of that moment is that everything else goes away. If you can actually make yourself believe that this is the beginning, the middle, and the end right now, then all those things go away. And there was a lot I didn't want to think about.

I think maybe I was working something out—as though I was saying, "Now it's my turn to flail." Also, you're in control—it's like seizing control. You're in control, you're calling the shots. Maybe kids who feel the need to attempt suicide today feel that they don't have control in their own lives.

Anyway, I loved being at boarding school. It was great—

I was away from this mire at home. And I had a great time. But all the same, some of that year was this self-destructive period.

Yet nothing happened in the barn. I just crept down the ladder and went back to my room.

———

Heather recognized that basic need of children to have someone to talk to. Many therapists agree that young people in situations similar to Heather's have a great need to share their secrets with others. Keeping silent about such an extraordinarily heavy burden, they say, can cause a terrible sense of aloneness and isolation for a young person. That is why some therapists, and even some schools, now provide a place where kids have a chance to not only talk about, but to act out—through play with dolls or games—some of the turmoil going on in their lives. Such acting and talking can be an important way of defusing some of the tension. And, having defused such tensions, the literal and dangerous acting out, such as Heather was doing in that barn, will not need to occur.

Another point that bears mention is Heather's reference to the need to have some "control" in her life. Therapists say that many young people in Heather's situation often talk about this need. It is as though they need to seize control in their lives because other things seem so totally out of control. As long as this "seizing control" is a positive one—taking control of one's personal or school life, exerting control over the length of one's hair or the manner in which one wears one's clothes—it can be a healthy, growth experience. It can be dangerous and ultimately futile, however, when one feels that the only way to gain such control is through deciding whether one will choose to die.

———————

Q: Heather, did you really want to die?

H: No. Being as objective as I can now, looking back on it, I can only say that I know I didn't want to kill myself. But I know it was self-destructive behavior, as well as maybe a subtle bid for attention, too.

Q: It seems as though you were able to work that out?

H: I did get help that worked, years and years later. At first I got a therapist who was sort of a—I don't know, just "feel good about yourself" and all that. I didn't need that. I needed some dynamite. And when I found the right one, he helped me find some things about myself. He was very skilled. I'd have these revelations. He'd set it up so I almost had to trip over these things in the dark. It was a very good relationship because I could discover the things myself. You have to find the right person at the right time.

Q: Do you think that *anyone* could have reached you the first time? When you were so little?

H: Yes, I do. But the first one wasn't geared for children. My mother thinks he was great. He was—for her. But I think you really have to have someone who's specifically tuned in to children. Who can appeal to their good side. He was looking for the bad stuff and I wasn't going to give it to him. Children are just naturally full of goodness. They want you to see the good first.

Q: Before they'll give you anything else?

H: Yes. So I think someone geared to children is so important.

Q: Could you talk about how things are with your relationship with your sister today?

H: Well, she married young. And then she had another nervous breakdown. She's had a hard life—illnesses and all. I've tried. But she just doesn't talk to me anymore.

When Heather refers here to a "nervous breakdown," she is using a term rarely used by professionals anymore. The term came into being because it was once thought that people who suffered from feelings of inadequacy, fatigue, loss of energy and memory (all the symptoms we commonly associate with nervous breakdown) were actually suffering from a breakdown or exhaustion of the nervous system— hence, "nervous breakdown." In fact, this is a catchall term that can mean anything. Most commonly, people use it, as did Heather here, to refer to a condition suffered by an individual who becomes mentally unable to function normally, and who requires either hospitalization or other intensive forms of mental health care.

Though the term "nervous breakdown" doesn't really mean anything anymore, there are entire classifications of mental illnesses, just as there are different classifications of physical illnesses. It matters less what the illness or condition is called than that a professional is able to adequately diagnose the condition and prescribe appropriate treatment.

H: So with my sister, there's always been this deep-seated jealousy. She feels that I've always had everything. She's always ridiculed me. In school, my best subject was languages. She'd say things like, oh, that's just memorization. And I'm an artist—I love to draw, I paint. She'd say things like, that's just hand-eye coordination.

My father really played up this good-girl thing with me, making everybody else feel less. What I was really was a pawn. He just played one person against the other. He's a really destructive person. For instance, when he and my sister were having a fight—they've always had this incredibly violent relationship—he'd have me come in to be the arbitrator.

So I guess I felt guilty because I was favored. Because of that, I'd always make the effort toward my sister. Yet I always felt like a yo-yo, coming and going on other people's whims.

When I finally said this to my sister, she got really irate. Said things like "How can you do this to me—after all I've been through?" She was always blackmailing people.

Q: Is that something you think she was doing with the suicide attempts?

H: Oh, yes. Suicide is the ultimate blackmail.

———

This is a very important statement that Heather makes—that suicide is a form of blackmail. There is no doubt that some individuals die by suicide out of overwhelming pain and inability to cope, but Heather is referring to a well-known psychological fact—that at least some people who kill themselves, and perhaps many more who attempt to, do it to gain something from others.

The blackmail statements can be many. By making an attempt on one's life, one may be trying to say, "If you don't treat me differently, I will die." Or perhaps, "If you make me suffer, I'll make you suffer more." Or even, "Look at what you've done to me." Regardless of what the statement is, many therapists would agree with Heather that suicide is the ultimate blackmail.

These individuals are not necessarily *deliberately* manipulative. They may be simply young people who, as Kelly said in an earlier chapter, feel they have just run out of any other way to cry for help. It may be that by saying, "I'm going to kill myself if things don't change," these young people feel, however mistakenly, that they will be able to effect that change. And many times, it is not a conscious decision, but an unconscious motive that is at work.

Whatever the motive, it is certainly a foolhardy form of blackmail, and most often, futile. When one is dead, one can no longer change anything—self or others.

Q: It must have been so scary to you as a child, Heather. You said you felt responsible?

H: Not *then*. But what happens is, you try to do as much as you can—*which is nothing*—so you just have to be the best person you can be. This awful thing has happened, even though at the time I didn't think I had anything to do with it. What I had to do was be the best person I could be. But you know, I felt so responsible, trying to do everything. It's this awful presence always there—this threat of her doing this again.

Q: Did you worry about it?

H: I don't remember it a lot, but I do remember once in the middle of class, just bursting out crying—crying so hard that I had to go home. But I don't remember exactly what I was thinking.

Q: What could you suggest doing for a child—a sibling who might be coping with a similar situation? Maybe something that would have helped you?

H: Find someone you can talk to, someone who senses and knows your needs. And find out that many people have had your experience. I remember for the longest while that

I didn't tell anyone because I wondered how it would reflect on me. What would people's reaction be? That might make it even worse. Also it would make it more real—God, it was real enough! So it would have to be someone who would know the needs and reactions of a victim—a child victim.

In the volatile situation I was in, I learned that these involvements are dangerous—talking leads to fighting, to violence. So talking wasn't a natural thing for me.

Q: That must have been scary—feeling that talking and violence were connected.

H: I remember sitting, listening, and this feeling would just come in my stomach when I would hear people start to fight. One night, I did leave home in the middle of the night and went to my best friend's house. It was only about a mile away, but it was night. I was just a little kid. But it was a refuge to be able to go to that house. My best friend was very important to me. Not that I ever told her anything. Except once, I told her that my parents were *thinking* about divorce. And that was long before they even divorced. But that's all I ever told her. Yet just having the comfort of that friendship and being able to go to that house was so important.

Q: Not even to talk? Just to be there?

H: Yeah. That's what I was thinking before when you asked what can you do for a child. The thing you *don't* want to do is have them feel they're being singled out— they feel they're being singled out already. What they really want is to be held. To feel that they're a part of a family. Because their family is being torn apart.

You know, with all the loss that was going on in my family—my brother in trouble, my father and mother getting divorced, this stuff with my sister—still my brother always wanted my help. We would fight, but still he'd want my help. Because that role that I was given of helper, good person, or whatever—well, essentially that part of me really existed. In the long run, once I got it in perspective, once I got it to work for me, then it was helpful.

Q: It's interesting that you're an artist.

H: That was my world. To sort of go into. I learned to paint and draw, to be home on summer days when I could have been at the pool swimming. I know I was drawing an awful lot by the time I was in sixth grade. I remember one afternoon my mother and I watched *Lust for Life*—the Van Gogh movie—that was a pretty tragic movie, watching this guy kill himself! Anyway, my mother offered to buy me a set of oil paints. And I went to the store and got the paints and I started painting.

Art always helped. I remember once when my parents separated and we moved, I wound up doing lots of collages. Spent days cutting out images from magazines, and putting them together in significant relationships.

———

When Heather says, "Art always helped," she again hits upon a well-known psychological fact. Many therapists, as well as researchers in the field of creativity, say that the individual who is able to find constructive, creative means of expressing him/herself, is frequently more able to cope with life stresses than the individual who has not yet found such means. Even Sigmund Freud, the father of psychoanalysis, saw creative writing as an extension of the play of childhood. Such release through creative expression or "play" is found not only in writing, or in Heather's field of art and drawing, however. It is also true of many other creative processes that young people may undertake—music, dance, theater, to name but a few.

In addition, it would be a mistake to think that only

such *traditionally* creative fields provide outlet for expression, and therefore release of personal tensions. Such diverse activities as team sports, running or jogging, stamp collecting—all are other positive outlets that exist for the creative channeling of one's feelings.

One ought to be cautious, however, if one finds a young person totally absorbed in any single activity. For example, some young people with suicidal tendencies have been known to spend great amounts of time writing about their suicidal feelings, and even showing these writings to teachers and friends. Unfortunately, it is only after the person has died by suicide that others see in such writings some "warning signals." The point here is not that such writing is healthy or unhealthy. Rather, any kind of activity that is carried to extremes or is used to signal a great personal distress ought to serve as a warning signal.

———————

H: I don't have any of my paintings that I did when those crazy times were going on. Every time my mother moved, she got rid of more and more stuff. So I have no traces of my past anymore. That irks me. Still, she had to do what she had to do. To save herself.

I get along very well with my mother right now. We're very compatible. My father was the one who was so destructive, who needed to get under the skin, who had to break people.

Q: Do you think you work out things in your art?

H: Yes, though it took me a long time. I've always worked from photographs because I like the privacy of a studio, I like working alone. But I didn't like my paintings. I guess I didn't like my paintings till I was quite grown up—till I liked myself, I guess.

It became a goal for me to be able to do painting *from* me, without having to look at photographs. It was very important for me to develop expression, just pure expression of myself. I took a series of photographs when I went to California, wonderful landscape photos that I wanted to work from. But what I wanted to paint was *not* what I was seeing in the photograph. The image in the photo reminded me of the *feeling* I wanted to capture. I wanted to use what I saw in a photograph as a takeoff point.

But I found myself just rendering these same paintings over and over again. I got better and better at it, but it was not what I wanted to do. I did not want to paint a mountainside!

I even had titles for all of the pictures I wanted to paint. They all had to do with: Where do I stand? One of them was a cliffside. I wanted to get the feeling of not having any place to stand. And I just kept on painting.

Eventually, I let go of my conscious, I guess. I stopped using my eyes so much. And I finally did it. It was the most important thing that I've ever done. Birds. And the people. Those were really important to me. In some paintings I was trying to express the feeling of powerlessness—because I had been powerless for so long. Those were really, really important paintings to me. It was grueling to get to that point. But once you've gotten there, you don't go back. And it will never go away.

It's like what you do in therapy. Once you've made that step, you can't go back.

Q: When you were talking, I kept thinking of the expression that that kind of art is like making a leap of faith?

H: Yes!

Q: Do you think your experiences as a child influence your art? Even the bad things?

73

H: That's such a good question. I've read articles saying that so much of literature and art today is self-interest motivated, getting these very personal things out—what-happened-to-me-when-I-was-young type of thing. And I read another that speculated about whether the artists of today are as good as the artists of history. Because today's artists don't have any big traumas behind them, and the artists of history had these monumental things like world wars. But I think we're in a different time and there are wars going on—but the wars are going on in the home.

Would I be the artist that I am had it not been for *my* history? No, I don't think I would be. Because it's too hard. I wouldn't agonize over these paintings if I didn't know I would be a better person for it afterward.

Q: It's almost as if you have to have had something that drives you, that needs to be expressed? The good and the not-so-good?

H: Yes. But you have to get past the "journal" stage. And then express it.

———

It has been said by others that one must get beyond one's individual feelings, must transform one's feelings so that they become relevant to the feelings of others, before one can create true "art." Such transformation is what differentiates art from what Heather called the journal stage—that is, the stage of simply *reporting* feelings and experiences. It is the artist's job to make those feelings meaningful to others, so that others can identify.

The experience of "identification" with an artist or writer has probably happened to each of us. Repeatedly, in books, movies, TV dramas, we are able to identify with the author's or artist's feelings, even when we've not actually lived through

the event. Feelings are universal. The artist's ability to relate those feelings in a meaningful way can bring understanding and awareness to viewers or readers. But in addition, the very act of creating this work of art or theater
or drama can be a positive, healthy experience for the artist
him/herself.

Q: I wonder about kids and art. Do you think art or
writing would help young people who are depressed or sad?
I don't mean art therapy necessarily, but providing some
way to express themselves?

H: Definitely. And I don't think art therapy is such a
bad idea, either. It's a great way to communicate.

I've just begun teaching art to kids. And I see that they
start learning so young to be embarrassed by what they put
on paper! It's such a challenge to get them to loosen up. I
see them just sitting there and they can't put anything
down. And so I ask them, "Do you ever get a picture in
your mind, and then you go to put it down on paper, and
it doesn't come out the way you saw it in your mind?" And
they say, "Yeah!"

So I say, "It's not going to hurt you to start. The line
is like a piece of clay, you can move it, it's not indelible.
It's not going to be wrong or bad." I tell them we're going
to draw a dog. Don't be precious with paper. We've got lots
of paper.

They say, "I don't know how to draw a dog."

I tell them that all a dog is is a hunk of fur, four legs,
and a tail. And I saw one kid. He just put down a blob—
but you know, it had gesture. And he said, real doubtful,
"I don't know about this." But it was great! Just sort of a
profile, sort of slumped, with a hump on its back. And all

at once, I was thinking, you *can* get kids to make that leap of faith. It's really wonderful. They want to trust you. And if they trust you they'll do it. And they'll benefit from it.

So I would say definitely to kids to do something to express what they're feeling and going through. I like to work with drawings. But for kids, the important thing is that they do *something*. If they feel intimidated by painting, then do something else—collages, whatever. Something artistic—because it will help.

———

There were many things happening in Heather Falk's life that might have been causes for depression—feelings of responsibility and guilt and isolation. Yet Heather survived this difficult situation—she called it a "mire"—and, in spite of some difficult times along the way, survived it rather well.

The question is sometimes asked: What makes one teen with seemingly overwhelming problems such as Heather's go on to struggle through and survive, while others, whose problems may appear less difficult, sometimes decide to end their lives?

According to researchers, one difficulty in answering that question is that what may seem like a small or manageable problem to one person may seem overwhelmingly difficult to another. This is particularly true if the other is trying to cope in the midst of a depression.

Therapists also say that what sometimes appears to be the cause of an individual's suicide is not, in fact, *the* cause. Occasionally one hears statements such as: "He didn't get into the college of his choice so he killed himself; she broke up with her boyfriend so she decided she couldn't live any longer." According to some therapists, sometimes such rejections *are* the triggering fact—the final straw, one might say. But rarely is it one thing that leads to a suicide. Rather it is a number of things, small and large, that seem to build and eventually form a crushing burden.

The ability to communicate is one distinguishing factor between survivors and victims. According to that criterion, Heather had an advantage—her mother did have her see a psychiatrist, and although Heather felt it wasn't the kind of help she could relate to, the fact is, the opportunity was there if she so desired. Even more important, however, Heather's mother, by making that help available to her, was indicating that she recognized Heather's needs and was in her own way attempting to fill them. Not perfectly, perhaps. But attempting. (And no one has ever said that parents or others who would help troubled individuals must be perfect themselves. Only that one does what one can.)

Other teens, even those interviewed in this book, also have had help available, have had supportive parents, and yet went on to cope with serious suicidal preoccupation and even suicide attempts. So the question remains: Why does one young person choose suicide, when another, in an apparently equally awful situation, struggles on? Why does one become seriously, dangerously depressed, while another suffers only from a moderately troubling sadness?

Even among researchers and therapists who study such things, there seems no single answer. Certain elements in individuals do may make them less vulnerable to suicide—and a creative outlet, such as Heather had, is one such sign. Other hints that may indicate an individual less vulnerable to suicide than others are included in Chapter 9.

According to some therapists, then, those like Heather who are able to express their inner life—in words, or by drawing, painting, dance, whatever—are much less vulnerable to suicide than those who have no outlet for their feelings.

This is probably not new. And it's probably not news.

But in all the clamor that often surrounds the issue of youth suicide, it seems sometimes that certain obvious things are overlooked. How obvious—and helpful—to recognize that each person has a basic need for some creative outlet for feelings.

In no way are these statements meant to suggest that access to the creative experience or creative outlet is *the* reason that some youths will choose life over suicide. It is only worth noting that creative expression is but one of many things that can enrich one, that can be a real contributor to mental health.

In talking with Heather, I could not help being influenced by her own belief and enthusiasm that art has enriched her life as well as her mental health. She experienced personally what has been recognized as a psychological truth.

Yet art and drawing and painting are not for everyone. What then could one do if one were not an artist? Practically anything that satisfies the creative urge will do—dance, sports, writing, music, collecting stamps or rocks or fossils. It really doesn't matter. As Heather said, "Do *something.* . . . It will help."

Chapter 7

Rachel, Megan, Sabrina, Allison, John, and Jeff

The Special Problems of Those Left Behind

This book would not be complete without considering the feelings and problems of those who are left behind—the other "victims" of a suicide. For each of the thousands of people who die from suicide each year, many, many more hurt and troubled friends and siblings and acquaintances are left behind. These young people are frequently depressed and puzzled. And when, as happens all too often, more than one friend or acquaintance in the same area or same school die by suicide, the survivors can be not only sad, but also worried and even sometimes frightened.

I met such a group of young people in the course of my research. All of them were members of a coed soccer team at a high school in a suburb of Boston, Massachusetts. In the few years that they had been in school together, they had lost several friends to suicide, and even more friends had tried to kill themselves. The most recent death occurred about two months before this taped session. It had happened during the last week of school, during final exam period, when a fifteen-year-old friend, Chris Anderson, killed himself by asphyxiation.

By far the most awful event these teens had experienced in their lives so far was that of losing a friend through suicide. There were so many factors and feelings involved: Was he trying to tell me something before he died? Did I miss something that I should have picked up on? Could I have prevented this death? Why isn't there anyone to talk to about it?

These are important questions to open up to readers. These young people bring a different perspective to the issue of youth suicide from those who were survivors of suicide attempts or of suicidal depressions. These were not young people who were deeply or even moderately depressed. They had thought about suicide themselves and rejected it. In addition, they had made some assessments of today's society and how it influences youth suicides.

They were an unusual group because they were so very close to and supportive of one another—possibly because of their close involvement with each other on the soccer field. They were also unusual because they were so tuned in to their emotional responses to what they had experienced.

There were six members of the soccer team present. Four girls—Rachel, Megan, Sabrina, and Allison. And two boys, John and Jeff.

They were asked to begin by talking about their feelings about their friends who had died—to use those as a takeoff point from which to explore other feelings and thoughts.

Rachel begins by referring to Chris, the latest suicide victim in their school.

———

Rachel: I didn't know Chris. But Megan, he was a friend of yours?

Megan: A good friend of mine. What was so weird is that he was so great. Girls were killing for him! He sat behind me in Algebra, and I'd always turn around and say, "Hey, Chris, what's going on?" And he *never* seemed unhappy.

Sabrina: He was the greatest guy. Everybody loved him.

Jeff: And nobody expected it from him.

Sabrina: I think sometimes the kids who are loved the most are the ones who have the greatest pressures on them to be the greatest people—to keep up that image.

Megan: One thing that Chris did—when his mother found him, he was in the garage, the door was open, and the car was turned off. I'm thinking that in the last minutes, he said, "I don't want to do this." He was found in the garage in a struggling position, as if he'd been running and fell—scratches on his face, where he fell—and that's why I think he thought: I don't want to do this anymore, I can stay around for a while.

Q: Do you feel angry or let down by him?

Sabrina: Disappointed.

Megan: If I'd heard he had family problems or pressures, I would say, well, I know where he's coming from. But I can't even *tell* what was going on in his mind. That's really what's bad—

Allison: The unanswered questions.

Sabrina: And you're annoyed at *him*. Because you think of what he did to everybody else. How could you do that?

Megan: And look at him, at a fifteen-year-old. If you think about it, a fifteen-year-old is just a baby. Any fifteen-year-old who thinks life just isn't worth living—well, there has to be something wrong with you in your head to do away with yourself. That's just not normal to have these thoughts.

John: The instinct is to survive.

Q: Yes, the instinct is to survive. But it *is* normal to have these thoughts. Don't you think it's important to say that?

Megan: Yes. The thoughts. But not to do it. What I don't understand about Chris is it was the end of the year. Five more days and then no more school. He'd have a summer of no more cares. It was the second day of exams. He was smart! He didn't have to worry about exams. So it couldn't have been pressures from school. I've been trying to figure this out ever since he did it. He had a girlfriend. Maybe that's it. Maybe he felt like she didn't care for him. But I don't know *why*. It seems like there *is* no reason why.

Sabrina: After he did it, we found out during class. Everybody was freaked out. And what we cried about was partly Chris, that he was dead. But also: Someone I was friends with is not here anymore. It's their fault. There's nothing I can do about it now. And it was just so scary knowing that.

Rachel: Right. It's not so much the person himself. I mean, even if I wasn't friends with him—even if I just knew who he was, still I would have cried for days. How could a person you know do that? I mean, it's just so close to you. Someone you are acquainted with takes his own life. That just brings it closer to yourself.

Sabrina: It was even hard to believe after I saw him at the wake. I was still saying, "But I don't understand."

Megan: The day after he did it, I walked into school

and everybody was buzzing around. My friend came up to me and said, "Guess what? Chris might have killed himself." I said, "Chris who?" And she said "Chris Anderson." And I said, "No! No, no, no, no! No way! No way!" I went up to class, and at the end of the period, they announced it on the intercom. You might think this was tacky, but it was good. It stopped a lot of rumors. People were buzzing around, saying he did this, he did that—

Q: What did they say on the intercom?

Megan: A student at our school took his life. Chris Anderson took his life. And that there would be a wake—

Jeff: And that we didn't have to take finals that day if we felt we couldn't.

Megan: The next day, I had to take an algebra final, and Chris had sat right behind me. Every time someone coughed or turned a page behind me, I kept thinking— Hey, it's Chris! And then I thought: No one is sitting there. And people were just staring at that chair. I could not concentrate.

Before the exam, the teacher said, "I'm sure we're all upset about Chris." And I cried for ten minutes. But some of the teachers really did not do very well for us—because they were just as upset as we were.

Jeff: All my teachers gave us an option not to take the exams, even those of us who didn't know Chris very well. That was great because—it's not whether or not you know the person. It's just that someone is gone. Whether or not you knew them, someone your own age, in your own situation, in your own town, is actually gone. He decided he wasn't prepared to live among you. And there's this feeling—

Sabrina: Of rejection—

Jeff: This weird thing comes over you for just a second: Maybe he's not so wrong. Maybe he did have a good reason.

But then if you think about it long enough—and the reason that most people stayed and took the finals—is that life has to go on. If a person wants to drop out of life, that's their decision. But you can't stray from your course. There is no good reason to kill yourself. Ever. You can always make a difference in the world.

Megan: Think about Chris's family. Can you see them looking at his chair at dinner—like everyone was looking at that chair behind me? I can't picture someone just *vanishing* from my dinner table.

Rachel: And at Christmastime when everybody comes home—

Megan: Chris has a little sister who idolized everything he did. I'm so worried for her.

Sabrina: I just freak out seeing that little kid and knowing that she's lost just so much.

Megan: Chris's best friend—Brian. They were so inseparable. Afterwards he wasn't crying—he was just sitting there—numb. Like plaster. And then at the funeral he began crying. I was so happy. I thought: Finally, it hit you. If it had hit him in the summer—like he thought: Hey, let's go sailing; I'll call Chris!—well, I'd hate to think of that happening to him.

Q: You've all had to cope with suicide already in your life. What would help you to cope better with the fact of suicide? Is there anything one could say that would help kids cope?

Sabrina: Maybe telling them that maybe the person is happier.

Several voices: No!

Rachel: But maybe someone seriously would rather have oblivion than pain.

Jeff: No! You can't let them think that.

John: People get together to talk about the person who

died, all the good things the person did. But I wouldn't be able to go to something like that. I wouldn't want to be reminded of what happened.

Sabrina: I don't agree. It's really good to talk about that person. We did that the day Chris died. We were in class, and the teacher came in with this lady—she's like a psychologist. We talked about how we knew him, and what we thought about it. It just made us feel so much better, getting it out of us. Just relating to each other and to him.

Q: Did you talk about the good and the bad?

Sabrina: Mostly the good, because mostly there were good things to say about him.

Allison: In our school, we have something called student educators, kids from high school who go talk to kids in junior high about drugs and alcohol and just high school in general. But no one ever came down and said anything about suicide. I think it should be brought up, by saying: This is a group of people you can talk to. And this is a problem and we realize it's a problem.

A lot of people haven't ever experienced suicide. Like me—I knew about it, but it wasn't a *real* thing until it *happened* to me.

Sabrina: It's like it can't be a name. It has to be a *face*.

Rachel: Well, that's true of any death. Do any of you *really* believe you're going to die?

Jeff: It only happens on the news.

Megan: I remember in eighth grade, a health class told us all about suicide. It began by talking about suicide—Latin definition as "self-kill." It was really good. It's sort of like having sex education in sixth grade—you just put it in the back of your mind and forget it till you need it.

Q: If someone came to your school to talk about suicide, what else would you want them to tell you?

Allison: That it's there and you *can talk* about it. To say something like this: My friend committed suicide and it can happen to you. Just to give it reality. Even if it just stays in the back of your mind. It's just like in sixth grade, after learning sex ed, you're not going to go out and have sex. But it's going to be in there somewhere.

Sabrina: You asked how to help kids cope. Well, we have kids to talk to. But sometimes that's a little hard. Sometimes what you need are adults to talk to. Because if you respect them, you figure they have stuff worth saying that's new to you, that you're not going to hear from another kid. After this thing with Chris, they decided at the school I went to that they were going to try something—you could choose one teacher you really feel comfortable with, and that will be your guidance teacher. So if you really need to talk with an adult, you can talk with that teacher. It's a really good system. If we'd had this before, we might have been a lot better off.

Q: You'd be more apt to go to a teacher you trust than a guidance counselor whom you don't see all that often?

Sabrina: Your guidance counselor is just—your counselor! Unless you like that person.

Q: But you would go to a teacher?

Rachel: Yes, definitely. But I couldn't just go up to a teacher and say, "Hey, I'm having a problem, could you talk to me?" Unless I was really, really good friends with that teacher.

Jeff: I would do it. I've done it before.

Q: Do you think maybe that the ones who die are the ones who don't have some special closeness—a special someone to talk to?

Megan: Chris probably thought that he couldn't tell his problems to people because people thought he was such a perfect person. So he didn't have anyone to talk to.

Jeff: That's a pressure in itself.

Rachel: He was the one who everybody went to with their problems. So if everyone went to him with their problems, who could he tell?

Megan: He couldn't go to anyone, because it wouldn't be like Chris.

Allison: I remember two other friends who attempted suicide—both times the first thing I can remember asking myself was: Did I miss something? God, were they trying to tell me something, and I wasn't even hearing them? They were having these problems, and was I so oblivious or so busy that I couldn't even hear them? My God, maybe if I could have talked to him, he wouldn't have done it. I think that was what really made me depressed. That's the worst—the what-if's?

Rachel: Same thing with my friend Susan—she showed me notes, but I didn't believe she would really do it. And when Paul, her boyfriend, called me and told me she'd tried to kill herself, he said she's okay now, she's fine now. Well, so what? She had tried to do it, and she was one of my best friends. What if I had really known, understood ahead of time, done something?

Allison: It's hard with friends. I came home from school one day, and my mother got me in the car and said we have to go to the hospital right away. My best friend had tried to kill herself and my mother said, "The only person she wants to talk to is you."

I got there, and the doctor said, "Well, she won't talk to any of us. She only wants to talk to you." The only thing they said to me before I went in was—"Please don't make her upset!"

(Laughter.)

Allison: So I walked in, and she's there. And—

Jeff: You don't know whether to smack them around for being so stupid, or—

Allison: What was I supposed to say?

Rachel: Oh, you tried to kill yourself this morning. So what else is new?

Allison: So I said, "Hi, how you doing?" Like, I knew she had gone out with this guy the night before who she really wanted to go out with. So I said, "So, did you have a good time?" And it's so awkward!

Rachel: With me, there was my friend, Marcia. She tried to do it in *my* house! I felt mostly bad for her, that she felt so bad that she wanted to do it. But in a way I was also mad at her for doing it there. It put pressure on me. At the same time, I was glad that she felt she could come to my house for help. I don't think she really wanted to die.

Jeff: I was really apprehensive about meeting Marcia after I heard about it. When Rachel brought her over, like that night at the movies, I didn't sit next to her.

Rachel: That was why?

Jeff: I was scared.

Q: I guess we all feel awkward in situations like that. Yet everything I've read says that if you have a friend who's thinking about suicide, or who you even *think* is thinking about suicide, you ought to talk about it.

Rachel: Yes, but when I was researching for a report I was doing on teen suicide, it said *don't* give the person who's suicidal reasons to live. Because they've already thought of all the reasons, and they'll just shoot down every one of yours. And I don't know what else to say.

Q: Maybe you could start with something like, "Are you feeling so sad that you're thinking of dying?" But I do know this: Don't take on the responsibility for saving that person. Get adult help. People will tell you in confidence— has this happened to any of you?—that a friend will tell you in confidence that he or she is thinking of committing suicide?

Several answers: Yes!

Rachel: Andy. He came to my house at Christmas after he broke up with his girlfriend. He said, "Don't tell anybody, but I've seriously thought of suicide." *Thought*. Past tense. He said don't tell anyone. But what are you supposed to do? *You've got to tell somebody!*

Jeff: I'd tell somebody immediately. I don't think it's your responsibility to try and save him. I think what we really need to know is that life is worth living. That when this kind of thing happens, it will be okay. You shouldn't take it upon yourself to feel everything about this person who died. You're not going to stop the pain. What we really have to know is that when it happens, *we* can survive. Even though that person felt that they couldn't.

Q: And things do get better.

John: There's a lot of things that show that life is worth living.

Jeff: I think one problem is the way TV and movies and all the media portray that everything in our world is supposed to come so easily.

Rachel: Like all the sitcoms. Every problem gets resolved at the end of the half-hour.

Jeff: Exactly. Everybody expects that their life is going to be the same. And when in real life something doesn't go right, you figure: Maybe there's something wrong with me. I'm causing my own problems. And the only way to get rid of that, is to get rid of me.

Q: Here you're all talking about others—pressures and problems that other kids have. But have any of you thought about suicide?

Jeff: Only in this way: that it would cause a lot of guilt. I would never do it. But thinking about it, I would never do it to *kill myself*. It's not a case of ending your own life. It's a case of destroying everybody else's. And it's the only time I've ever thought of it. You know how you think: "I'll bet if I was gone they'd feel differently."

All: Yeah.

Q: So there's some element of punishing others in your thinking?

Jeff: It's a way of hurting other people through your pain.

Sabrina: But thinking about others might also hold you back from doing it.

John: Sometimes there's a different reason, the feeling of wanting to end it all. No more problems. But then you start to think: There's nothing else. There's no more problems, but there's no happiness, either. There's nothing.

Rachel: Like in two weeks you might win the lottery and be rich and famous. And get your Porsche! I've never thought of it seriously. But I'd never do it to punish. When I've thought of it, I've only thought in terms of *getting away* from something.

John: Sometimes things get bad. One thing happens, then others happen—

Allison: Exactly. It always seems like it all piles on at once.

Megan: But then you can go for months with no cares.

Jeff: You have this triggering thing—then you begin to notice all these other things around you that aren't working out.

Rachel: Things piling up.

John: But I think of life as a gift—not in a religious sense—but when you think of all the odds that it took just to get you *into* this world. That your grandparents had to get together and then your parents, and so many factors involved. Once you're here, it just seems that you're throwing away that gift if you choose to die.

I don't know if I've ever really seriously considered it.

Besides thinking of life as a gift, I don't have the guts. I fear death. It's just total oblivion. I don't know what's there.

Allison: I think a lot of kids around here have a lot, compared to others. Good schools, and most of us get the use of our parents' cars, and—

Q: But so many kids who have so much are choosing suicide.

Allison: Exactly. I don't think they have the same appreciation for life as someone who doesn't have all these things. Maybe those who really have to fight to make their life worthwhile have a lot more appreciation for living than those who are handed everything.

Q: That maybe your peers have too much?

Allison: I wonder.

John: Maybe I have a pampered existence, but it doesn't seem to me that things could get so bad that I'd risk everything to go into some unknown.

Megan: Two years ago, when I was in eighth grade, I was thinking about suicide. It seemed as if I was just living up to what other people wanted me to be. But then, after a while, I thought: I *am* doing these things for myself. I *want* to be doing what I'm doing. I *want* to be vice-president of the school, singing in the chorus, all that. And it changed my mind.

Allison: I think also about what Jeff just said—about things piling up, the feeling of being a failure. I find myself in that situation a lot. You really bust yourself to write a paper or try to get good grades or something. To write that paper and get it back and get a C, knowing that you really tried. Or you do something to please your mom, and she's just like—shrug. And you see that something you really tried at means nothing. It just makes me feel really bad. You're trying to make *other* people happy, and it doesn't work. It always seems to happen all together, all at the same time. As if you just can't get anything right. And you think, my God, if I can't do anything to make anyone else happy—

Jeff: Then what's my purpose?

John: Suicide gets glamorized, too, you know that? In the media, surprisingly enough, suicide gets glamorized. Like the recent TV movies about teen suicide.

Jeff: They're so ridiculously sugary.

Allison: They showed that kids couldn't have what they wanted, so they killed themselves.

Q: Did they make suicide seem more appealing?

Jeff: They didn't make it seem more appealing. But they didn't make it seem *less* appealing!

Allison: They didn't put it down or anything.

Jeff: They didn't make any point. They just took a bunch of facts and shoved them in your face. I think the Billy Joel video—"You're Only Human (Second Wind)"—makes more of a point about suicide than anything else. And it's only three minutes long.

Rachel: It's great. It shows a kid about to jump off a bridge and he's looking at a picture of his girlfriend, and he's all sad. Billy Joel shows him what it would be like if he died. Then he shows what it could be like if he lived. Future life.

Jeff: It gives him the two options. But it glamorizes living.

Rachel: At the end, the kid realizes. And he goes back.

John: It just shows that you have to wait. You have to wait till your second wind comes along.

Jeff: It's the only thing I've seen in the media that actually says anything true about teenage suicide. Or at least glamorizes life.

Q: What do you think about statements that some songs glamorize suicide? Blue Oyster Cult and their song "Don't Fear the Reaper"?

Megan: I think that stuff is garbage.

Jeff: I think music is whatever you want to make it to be. You can take anything in two veins. Really. Especially Blue Oyster Cult, who I happen to think is a pretty talented group of people. They write songs, and everybody says they glamorize death. But they also glamorize life. Nobody takes a look at both sides.

What I'm saying is, if you want to commit suicide, you're going to commit suicide whether there's a song about it or not. It's not a song that you're going to be listening to and suddenly you say "Hey! Let's commit suicide." It doesn't just happen like that. That's not going to induce suicide.

Rachel: No, but it could influence your decision. I think that if you were thinking about committing suicide already, and you heard a song that glamorized death it could influence you toward it.

John: A lot of the songs, I think, aren't just glamorizing death itself. I think what they're trying to do is just give everybody a message not to fear it so much. They're not saying to go out and kill yourself. They're saying live your life to live your life. Don't fear death and ruin your life like that.

Q: Could we sum up some of your thoughts about the issue of young people and suicide?

John: The thing that's so terrible about suicide is that for a teenager life's just started.

Rachel: It's so awful to stop life—when it's just beginning.

Jeff: All a teenager knows yet is school and friends and family. A teenager doesn't know anything about the outside world.

Sabrina: You kill yourself now, even though you're so depressed, you think of what you're going to miss.

Allison: You see all these shows about teen suicides, and you think: It happens. But the first time it happened to me, someone who did it and succeeded in killing himself, it smacked me in the face. It's like—it really happens to you, and to people around you.

Jeff: And it does happen. But the one thing that makes me feel better in that situation, the thing that helps, is to know that somewhere there is someone who will hold you. Who will tell you it's going to be okay. Who will just be there for you. There is nothing you can do to stop the pain. You've just got to feel it. And if you feel it immediately, and if you're with somebody who cares about you . . . it just makes it easier.

————

I think these young people were making some extraordinarily strong statements concerning their lives. They had looked at the issues of life and death, considered the suicides of their friends and what the consequences were, and they had said: This is not for me. They looked at the influence of TV and movies and rock music, and came up with conclusions. Their conclusions may be different from one another's. And perhaps different from the conclusions of those who may read this book. What is important is that they were thinking—clearly and, unfortunately, with a great deal of sad experience.

Chapter 8

The Parents of David, Diane, and Peter

A Message from the Parents of Suicide Victims

In some ways, this chapter may be the saddest, since those who speak are parents of those who are gone, who are unreachable, who can no longer be saved.

When I undertook to interview parents of young people who had died by suicide, I thought they might have important insights that no one else could contribute. Yet I also realized that certain teens view parents as their adversaries and might be unable to really *hear* what parents have to say, no matter how valuable those insights might be.

Yet almost all the young people I interviewed agreed that—although family problems were certainly a big part of their lives—parents, as well as other adults, had important, worthwhile things to say. Sabrina, in the previous interview, emphasizes just that—that adults you respect have something to tell you that another kid just can't.

Certainly the parents left behind would have something to say that a kid, or even another adult, could not. Since the parents were the ones most involved on a day-to-day basis, perhaps in hindsight they would see things they might want to point out to others. Perhaps they might have a message—one that, because of their experience, would be more easily heard and recognized by young people coping with their own self-destructive urges.

And so I undertook the interviews. The courage of the parents who volunteered their time to talk with me, who spoke freely, oftentimes through their tears, is an experience I will not soon forget. Nor will I forget that these parents were not only willing to talk, but also were eager to talk—because they wanted desperately to help others. They wanted to help other parents who were coping with similar tragedies. They wanted to help other young people whose friends had died. But most important, they wanted to talk to young people in the hopes of persuading them to choose to go on living.

I chose one interview that seemed most typical of the emotions and thoughts expressed by the others. At the end, I have included comments from several other sets of parents, interviewed at different times and places, all of whom had lost a son or daughter to suicide. No parent claimed to have an edge on wisdom. None claimed that their own experience was necessarily that of other parents. But there were common feelings expressed—fear and pain and second-guessing. As well as tremendous hope and optimism for the future.

Katherine and Pete Mallison met with me in the home of their brother, with whom I had become acquainted during the course of my research for this book. Pete is a hospital administrator for a large hospital in the Southeast. Katherine is a physician. Their son David fatally shot himself a few years previously.

A unique feature of this interview is that I was privileged to receive from the parents a letter written by their son shortly before his death. The letter illuminates the difference between the inner and outer person we encounter when faced with a youth who has suicidal feelings. Here were two concerned, conscientious parents, who obviously loved and cared for their son. The young person they described was a handsome young man of accomplishments, loving, caring, a success in the world, surrounded by friends. His view of himself was a different one entirely. His was a view of despair. "Everyone I see has qualities I wish I possessed," he wrote. "I can't find one redeeming quality in my own life."

Yet his life was full of redeeming qualities. His personality and drive were such that the family joke was that David would be president of a major corporation by the time he was thirty. His mother talks of the many friends he had. His father tells about a special nickname given to David by his friends—a nickname meant to denote one who is loving and caring and honorable.

Yet David did not know—really know—about the love and strength of his family and friends. Nor did he believe in his own fine qualities. He was overcome with feelings of genuine despair.

"Mom, Dad and all the other people in my life," he wrote. "Why couldn't I feel love when others loved me? Am I hopeless? I think I am."

His parents did everything imaginable to help. Although he was in enormous pain, he was not unreachable. As his mother says, "He just didn't give himself enough time."

And that, perhaps, is the reason each set of parents allowed themselves to be interviewed: the hope that their experiences might allow even one person to think it over again, to seek out someone who might help. To allow even one person to buy some time.

In the following interview, I used the initials "M" for David's mother and "F" for his father.

M: My anxiety is such that I want to talk right away, if you don't mind. Someone asked once if David showed any of the traditional signs of potential suicide. People talk all the time about signs—a great personal loss, change of personal appearance, giving away possessions, sudden gain or loss of weight. But for our son, there weren't any of those signs. And I think that's true, not only for him, but for a lot of other kids. I know I find that true in my experience as a physician. I think it's misleading, because sometimes there are *none* of those symptoms. Nobody seems to say that. And we have to point that out.

You'll get a sense from the letter David wrote shortly before he died of how helpless and hopeless he felt. Yet there were none of the hard signs.

F: But there was absolute evidence that he was seriously depressed, going back for a period of a few months before he died. We started to get calls from him from college, sometimes in the middle of the night. And he would cry. About all kinds of things.

M: He had this inner turmoil about his relationship with others, his inability to make everything "nice."

F: We brought him home from college for a time after

the phone calls. But after a while we felt he could go back.

M: There were other phone calls. We brought him home a second time. He was home for about eight weeks. From Labor Day until the day he died.

Q: Did he get any help?

M: We got psychiatric care for him. We gave him the option of which therapist to go to. David always talked a lot to me. He'd even follow me around, room to room. Communication was never a problem for him. But depression was. And I think it is for other kids.

When we first brought him home, like the physician that I am, I had him checked over by another doctor. I knew there can be other things, physical things, that can cause depression. We found him well, even though he kept complaining of all sorts of things. That's another symptom that nobody mentions, and it ought to be mentioned as a real warning signal—preoccupation with self. Some kids don't know why they feel so terrible, so they try to identify physical problems. For example, he went through things like "I can't keep my shoulders straight, I can't keep them back." Or, "I can't breathe out of my nose." So we sent him to a nose-and-throat person. And his posture—he had beautiful posture. But we had it all checked out anyway. There was nothing physically wrong with him.

Also, he didn't think he was attractive. But later I'll show you a picture of him. He was very good-looking. And at school, everyone looked up to him.

F: Every school that David went to, people gathered around him. He was everyone's idol. Do you know what his nickname was in college? "Lance," for Sir Lancelot, the noblest of King Arthur's knights. He was very thoughtful. He hated any kind of inequity, not only against himself, but anyone. In retrospect, there was this sensitive side of him that we just took for granted.

M: But maybe that in itself is one of the keys—when

people are too sensitive to others and to their own feelings. They think they can never live up to others' expectations.

Q: Do you know what caused that final decision?

M: I've wondered what happened that day. So much is said about the fact that a lot of times when a person kills himself, he's on the way up. That he has the strength to do it. The night before David died, he had been to his psychiatrist. I asked him that night about the visit to the doctor, and asked whether the doctor had given him medicine. He said no, the doctor said he was getting better.

I later found, on the phone bill, that the day he died he had made a lot of phone calls—to his friends, his girlfriend. Afterward, his friends blamed her. But I don't feel that was the case. I think it was other things—he internalized other people's problems. I think he just didn't give himself time.

Q: Had his girlfriend broken up with him?

M: She was leaving for another school and he was very upset about it. And she was going out with other people.

F: We can't underestimate other things that were happening, though. A few days before, we wanted him to go to an affair for his cousin—he and his cousin had been close. But he said, "No, you go ahead, I'll stay home." I got annoyed with him. I said, "You know, you're being a little selfish." I got so upset, I left the house. And then he went to his mother, his brother, and said, "Where's Daddy? Go find Daddy." Because he was so upset about what happened. So I came back. But I've felt terrible about that ever since.

My son was in a deep depression, with all a deep depression does to one. I'd say, "We're concerned about you." Or I'd say things like "You have everything in the world going for you." But that would just make him mad. And we tried everything. Everything, everything in the world.

It was a few days later that I found the suicide note on the kitchen table. He didn't say he was going to kill himself. But he said good-bye. He said I'm sorry. And that he was going away.

After he died—I have a friend in the medical examiner's office. After the autopsy, he called me and he said there was no evidence of drugs. I hadn't even *thought* that he was taking drugs. It's amazing how when people hear about these things they come to you and ask if David was involved in drugs. At least I was happy to be able to say, no, he wasn't. But that doesn't make the fact that he's gone any easier.

M: He had so many friends. The line around the funeral home went for blocks with all of his friends. In that letter, you'll read how friendless he felt. And you'll not believe it.

F: I had an important position and the police did not give this information to the papers. Because of my position, the only thing that ever appeared in the paper was "died suddenly, at home." We were blessed by that, by not having "suicide" appear in the papers. It must be an awful experience for the parents to have it in the paper and on TV. The media tend to dramatize it. Sometimes they mislead people about it. I know that papers have a responsibility to report news. I just wish there were a way to take a more ethical approach in reporting suicide. It's bad enough to lose your child.

Q: Is there anything you might say to parents of young people who seem similarly depressed—or to kids themselves?

M: What I would say to parents of other young people is: We tried everything; for our son it didn't work. But keep on talking to your young people. Tell them to talk—talk to their friends—

F: *Don't give up.* Keep on trying. There are kids who you can talk to. They're not all the same. We tried everything. But there are all different circumstances for families, different things to try.

M: I'd also say this to kids: There's a theory that depression is anger turned inward. So talk to your friends so your friends can be aware of your feelings. It can sort of give you a reality testing. Friends might be able to say that they, too, have been very depressed, but as time went on, things got better and life became worthwhile again. You know, some people mean well, but they say things like "Oh, this problem is nothing like such and such a problem." But loss is loss. I can't get inside your skin and you can't get inside mine. There's no way to *quantify* it. To a kid who's depressed, whether or not he finalizes it—it's real. And it's really bad. So communication is so important. And trying to get help is so important.

I also want to say something else. You know, afterward, a lot of people come to comfort the parents, and they forget about other kids in the family, that their pain is as bad. So I'd say, don't forget the others.

For our Tim, David's brother, the way he was able to resolve his grief was by going up to his brother's school and being around David's friends there for about two years. He stayed there and gathered everything he could about David's life. And he took David's motorcycle apart and stripped it down. That motorcycle had been a source of frustration to David because it didn't work, something he wanted to work so badly. Tim stripped it down to infinite parts, and built it back up again. So this is the first time, three years later, that it really works.

And also, and finally, I'd like to say this: As parents, we tend to hang on to the kids—to the friends of the one who died. Until you realize that the young people have to get on with their own lives. And then you have to give them up.

In interviews with parents, I was occasionally startled to hear one set of parents make statements that were almost identical to those of other parents. This was true whether or not these parents knew each other.

I was privileged to attend a meeting of a support group made up of several sets of parents, all of whom had lost a child to suicide. At that meeting, one mother and father talked about the outstanding quality of their fifteen-year-old daughter's life and accomplishments. In addition to being a loving, caring daughter and friend, she had been talented musically, intellectually, athletically.

"But," says her mother, "although Diane was good in all these things, *she didn't know it*. To her, she *wasn't* good. She had no self-esteem at all. No matter how much you told her about how wonderful she was, she didn't know it. She always had a plastic smile. Yet she *was* wonderful. Everybody loved her. The school people thought she was wonderful. All the kids loved her."

Perhaps the sense of worthlessness was the greatest similarity that parents mentioned. That worthlessness was felt by the young person regardless of the *reality* of that person's life. It was as though a silent theme played in the lives of all the young people who had died, a theme of worthlessness and despair.

Another issue raised repeatedly by parents was the role that friends can play in helping parents, as well as each other, after a young person's death by suicide.

The Mallisons made a point of asking friends to remember how much the siblings, as well as the parents, were hurting. Their plea was to ask friends to reach out to the brothers and sisters, also. A father at the group meeting wanted to speak directly to the potential readers of this book about the same issue. But his request was slightly different. "I want to say just one thing," he said. "And this is for kids. Since our daughter died, not one of her friends has come to talk to us. We know they're hurting—I'm not going to blame them. But I think, if they did come, it could be a help to someone else."

"It would help you?" I asked.

"It might help *them*," he replied. And then, "It might help both of us."

Another similarity that cropped up again and again was the lack of communication on the part of the young person who had died.

"Communication is everything," said Diane's mother. "Yet my daughter wouldn't tell me anything. But she was very creative. She would talk about *other* people having problems. When it was *her* problem she was talking about."

"Oh, yes!" said another mother, whose son, Peter, had also died. "My son did the same thing. Talked about other people."

"And I also remember," continued Diane's mother, "I remember thinking when Diane would tell me these things, 'Gosh, that poor person with all those problems.' When it was really *her* she was talking about. But she couldn't say 'me.' And I didn't realize. We did talk about suicide once. I went into Diane's room and she was reading a book by an author who had committed suicide. I remember saying, 'Why are you reading that? If you ever got to that stage, you would get help, talk to someone, wouldn't you?' And she said, 'Oh, Mom! I'm reading it for school. I'd never do anything like that!' "

"You're telling a parallel tale to mine," said Peter's

mother. "It's an important thing to point out to parents that if kids are talking about other kids' problems, they may, in fact, be talking about their own."

Do these parents think the open discussion of suicide today is a good or a bad thing? How do they feel about the open discussion of suicide in schools and society in general?

"Wonderful! Great!" were some of the comments. Almost all agreed that the groups in schools, the support groups, as well as suicide prevention information centers and suicide prevention programs, could be lifesavers for young people.

However, all parents objected to publicity about suicide that seemed to glorify it—or, as one father pointed out, that told one how to do it. "What I object to," he said, "is a segment I saw on a news program that told where one could write away for information on how to commit suicide. That is wrong. What's right is professional groups, not necessarily therapy, but groups that sit down and talk. What's right is groups that bring it out in the open—as opposed to advertising the damn thing."

He went on, "I think that if our daughter went to someone in her school today and said she had a real problem and was thinking of suicide, school personnel would be receptive to talking about it. And that, I think, is great. Kids need someone to reach out to. Parents will do anything—anything—to help their children. But sometimes kids will accept help from *other* people more readily."

His wife agreed. "I think," she said, "that if it were today, she might still be alive, because the climate in the schools is so different. When she died, no one was recognizing suicidal depression. I think it's good that it's being talked about."

Another point frequently made by parents was that the ultimate act of suicide was not, in fact, one isolated act, but the culmination of a depression and sadness that had been building for a long period of time.

One mother told of a poem she had written about her son years earlier. "He had beautiful eyes," she said. "An arresting feature. And I wrote about how the childhood had gone out of them, how the eyes were shuttered."

When she wrote that poem, her son was only eight years old.

"Look for it in their eyes" was a statement that many parents echoed. And when you see it, "Do what you can to get in there. Or get someone else in there to help."

Finally, and perhaps most tragically, again and again this point was made, by both parents and psychiatrists alike: If someone is hell-bent on killing himself, there is not always anything a parent can do to stop it. Try, yes. Try everything, yes. But if one's efforts are ultimately foiled, it is important to remember that only the individual himself or herself has made the final, ultimate decision.

The reason these parents agreed to talk, to live through their pain again, was their belief that although it is too late for their children, it's not too late for others. Other young people are still reachable.

Parents need to know that there *are* things they can do to help, that because one thing didn't work does not mean something else will not. One must keep trying. If one therapist does not work out, try another. If one form of therapy does not work, another might. If individual therapy doesn't work, perhaps family therapy will. If outpatient therapy does not work, perhaps hospitalization may be necessary to temporarily give a child the secure environment that is needed.

Another important point is that the individual who is talking about other people's problems may well be talking about his or her own. Those who are hurting can be extremely creative about hiding that hurt—while at the same time, sending out warning signals.

It was also important to hear parents expressing, from their own experience, what therapists and researchers have been saying is perhaps the most important sign of an individual who is seriously depressed—the sadness and sense of worthlessness. It is that lack of *knowledge,* on the part of the suffering individual, of the value and importance and goodness of his or her life, that ought to be a prime warning signal to a watchful parent. If parents hear or see such signs of lack of self-worth, they should take steps to intercede and get help if their child seems unable or unwilling to help him- or herself.

Sometimes one's own intuition is the best guide for knowing that a child is in trouble. As one mother said, her son was not showing any of the "typical" signs. He did not give away prized possessions; he did not gain or lose weight; he did not talk of suicide. Yet there were signs that she picked up on. Communication is crucial. Remember, one will never put the idea of suicide into someone's head by talking about it. In fact, just the opposite may be true, because the person may be very relieved to be able to share what is going on.

Finally, since this chapter is particularly about parents, it is a chapter that readers might want to share with their parents. Talking about what is going on, sharing one's concerns, showing that one cares enough to say, "I'm worried" may be the very thing that will help.

Chapter 9

Dr. Eleanor Craig

From a Therapist's Point of View

This chapter and this interview, perhaps more than any other, seemed to me to be a hopeful one.

I found, somewhat to my surprise, that therapists (and sometimes parents and researchers) were saying exactly what young people were saying. The language was perhaps somewhat different. But the facts were much the same—that stresses build to sometimes unbearable proportions, that one may be unable to cope if certain basic support systems have not already been established, that young people need to be heard. It was encouraging to know that those who can help are so much in tune with young people. Therapists know the kind of help—and listening—that young people are asking for. They know how important that help is. They know how to give it.

But perhaps most important, therapists can provide

interesting insights that those involved with their own pain cannot. Being an objective observer, a therapist is often able to sort out what an individual is really saying from what the individual *thinks* he or she is saying.

In an earlier chapter, Dr. Skowronski says something similar—that often a young person is saying, "Please hear what I'm not saying." That may sound like double-talk, but consider how many of us say one thing when we mean another: "I never want to see you again" can mean "You've hurt my feelings, and I want to hurt you." Such a statement is not all that different—except in degree of seriousness— from what Kelly said in an earlier chapter. "I'm going to kill myself," she said. But what she really meant was "I'm hurting so bad, please do something to stop me."

And so, it seems clear that therapists, with their training to really *hear* what another is saying, have something valuable and unique to contribute to this book.

I first learned about Eleanor Craig by reading several books she had written. She writes eloquently about her involvement as a therapist with young people. I sought her out not because of her reputation as a particular expert on youth suicide—although she has certainly worked with many teens who had suicidal feelings—but because her reputation went beyond that. She was known as a warm, caring, talented therapist with young people. She seemed able to see an entire individual, not just one hurting or sick aspect of that person.

I requested an interview with her, and we met at her offices in Westport, Connecticut.

———

Q: Could we begin by talking—not about teen suicide, but about teenagers and their feelings and emotions?

E: I think of all of us as being on a spectrum—sometimes I think of it as a tightrope—and I see either end of it as where we go at the most difficult times of our lives.

I always imagine *all* of us there because I don't like to separate out those who are in trouble at one time of their life from all of us who are on that continuum. Because I can get out there on either extreme, too—we all can.

So, way out there at one end are the times when we feel so angry that it's projected out—the acting-out side, where it's pushed out to other people. Over at the other end of the spectrum or continuum, there are the same feelings, but they're turned inward—sometimes because the kid can't turn against that person who seems to have wronged him or her because that person may be too powerful or strong. So then the anger goes inward toward self. Sometimes it's love turned into hate, and it seems there's no way out of this relationship. So those feelings are internalized and taken against oneself instead of released. And the person appears withdrawn—the most severe cases actually cease talking and moving and functioning.

Somewhere in the middle—I think of it almost as having parentheses around it—is something I call a comfort zone, where we all try to live or work. And we can zoom out to either end briefly.

Most of us can go out there and come back without any life-threatening intensity, and with only brief stays. But for some, the frequency and duration of being on the extremes are much, much greater. And for some, it's difficult to get back. Or they lose their way back. Or get stuck there. Kind of like a train getting off the track.

Q: It must be comforting for young people who are hurting to hear that—that it's temporary.

E: Well, if I were ill, I wouldn't like anyone to tell me there's no hope. We hear so much that phrase that gets thrown around—tunnel vision—where the person in despair doesn't see any other way out. And sometimes we all get ourselves into small situations, Catch-22 situations, where it seems as if there just isn't any alternative.

I heard a story from a doctor who worked with a girl who had jumped off a bridge, and the girl was able to report later that the minute her feet left the bridge, the minute she was airborne, she regretted it. She was sorry. And in some way she was able to turn her body and survive, although she was paralyzed. And I know another who leapt from a bridge onto a freeway, and she had somewhat the same experience—rolled and tried to save herself and survived with broken bones.

Q: So your message, then, is that suicides, would-be suicides, don't want to die?

E: Would-be suicides, those who have lived, whom I've met, at the last minute express doubt and regret about leaving permanently. With that tunnel vision, there's a sense of passing through to the better life that's going to happen. I think that's true of adolescents who are angry, especially at parents, and feel that in some way this self-murder is the murder of the incorporated parent. But also there is the fantasy that they will come back and reap the benefit of the grief and the new look at things that the parents will have experienced. So there will be this passing through, this idea that death is not final.

I think a lot of them think about or glamorize their own funerals—who will be there to mourn, and what it will be like, and how sorry everyone will be. And there's some sense of reaping the benefit of that sorrow. As if they'll be back to be treated differently.

I also think for some there's a wish to pass into peace.

And control is obviously an issue in adolescence. Because everything goes out of control. Here's a time of life when kids want to believe that they can make it in so many ways—academically, socially. And they can't always control those things. They're at a time when the one thing we all think we can control—our bodies—are rampantly out of control: hormones are flowing, breasts are developing, hair is growing, and so forth.

Parents get into terrible struggles over control with their kids. Parents make such a big issue about length of hair, but one of the few things kids *can* control about their bodies is their hair. You can't control how big some of the sexual parts of your body are getting.

Another way of getting control, of course, is with clothes. Young people are making statements with clothes. Parents get into struggles with that. And of course, every parent I know gets into the issue of how the room looks. And how much do you allow and how much don't you allow?

Sometimes the kids who have the most trouble separating, who are really the neediest, are the ones who are setting up the biggest battles. Parents feel it's just a total rebellion against them and a rejection of them. And yet, a lot of those battles are really because it would be so nice to be able to stay dependent.

Q: Why would that be—that the ones who are the neediest are the ones setting up the greatest battles?

E: Because the pull is so strong *not* to separate. So they have to do things like burn a hole with a cigarette in the coffee table, or do flagrantly violent things like punching a hole in a door. In order to get *kicked* out. Because leaving is so hard. I see kids asking to be kicked out because they don't dare leave on their own. And parents don't know whether to kick them out or let them back in or what.

There's a book I have that says it very well—"Hold them very close and let them go." So if we could do suicide prevention we'd do it very young, between the age of birth and two years old.

Q: How?

E: All the messages get programmed in. Trust, for instance. Who we are and our ability to relate to others get established right there at birth.

Q: Is it true—that young people who are showing signs of suicide are saying, "Save me"?

E: Yes, because you know, with suicide, it's not one decision. It's a spiral. Most people who think about suicide don't do it the first time. There are hints, gestures. And if you don't hear it, chances are it will be escalated. Getting help is critical. For me, if I hear those messages, I always talk hospitalization at that time.

If the family is not willing, I make them responsible for a twenty-four-hour watch until the person comes back.

Q: But that's scary, isn't it? To say: "Just because I'm thinking of suicide you want to hospitalize me."

E: I don't say it that way. I say: "I'm very concerned about you. And I don't think I can take good enough care of you. I'm not there all the time. I think you need people who are there for you all the time right now."

Q: Do you think that every young person who is thinking of suicide needs hospitalization?

E: I think you have to have a pretty good evaluation of exactly what's going on. One of the significant issues is: Has the person thought of how to do it? That's very important. If there's a plan, I certainly think you need some intervention.

Q: Isn't it important to say to a young person that just because you're thinking about it doesn't mean you're going to do it? It's not inevitable, you're not crazy?

E: Yes. Sometimes suicide is being toyed with, and there's a reasonable chance that the kid will listen and can be trusted—based on the relationship between the young person and the counselor—then it might help to make a contract with the person. It might go something like this: Promise me that before you do anything you will talk to me, we'll have another session. Maybe the person can call the counselor every morning, every night. Sometimes we have such a contract signed, witnessed, maybe by the parents, copies run off. We do all this to stress the seriousness of the contract.

Sometimes it helps to tell a kid who's in an intolerable situation and is looking at suicide as a way out that there are other ways out. If it is unbearable at home, it might help to get away—perhaps to a boarding school.

You see, in suicide, there's always an element of "getting" someone else. But it's not always totally self-murder or totally projected murder of another. Sometimes it's an unbearable situation, and it helps to point out options.

I've certainly told kids that their parents are sick. And that there's certainly something wrong with parents who can't love their kid or accept their kid. But is that a reason to give up hope that you can ever be loved? And that you can give love?

I suppose all of us need something in our lives to look forward to. And that's not always in young people's lives. So often kids feel that there's nothing to look forward to.

We cannot always prevent suicide. A person who is bound to commit suicide is going to find a way if he or she is absolutely determined. We have to work with the living. It's over for the suicide. But it's the people who have to go on who need help.

There's such rage involved. I mean, forget about suicide for a moment. Think about how you feel if you've been in a love relationship and the other person just walks out, never giving you a chance to express your feelings. Compounding the reality that he's walked out, that you'll never see him again, is the element, of course, of anger.

But in suicide, there's anger, not only from the person

who's left behind, but from the one who suicided. The more violent the act, the more anger there is toward the survivors.

There's so many reminders for a long time when one has lost people one loves through this kind of abandonment. There are so many anniversaries afterward—birthdays, and the times when you would have done such and so together. And the anniversary of the death itself needs to be used as a chance to reawaken the grief and let the person pass through it again more briefly.

I've been thinking about kids I've worked with and what they were trying to say by the suicidal gesture. One of them is still in a hospital, making suicidal gestures every time it's time to get out. She's done very well, she's proven her own insight, her ability to understand. But the truth is, she has nowhere to go. She's caught in a second marriage of a parent and she's unwelcome and has been since she was very young. Every time the hospital makes plans for her to go, she does other threatening behavior. I struggled to find another living situation for her, but it didn't work out. There is a tremendous need for a place for kids who can't make it through their adolescence in their own homes, but don't need a hospital. Of course, I try to intervene with the whole family. But it's only in the good situations when I can.

I'm working with another girl right now. Her mother had problems with her own mother who had died by suicide. But this family was workable. It was important to separate them and show them that they can have a good life and a trusting relationship. I can tell by their ability to relate to me, or mine to reach them, whether they can go out and relate to others.

It's important for kids to see their own part in a family, and what they can do, what they might have to defer for now, and how they can help make a family a family.

There are things that make a family a family. We all

think about "The Waltons," the old TV show where everybody says "Good-night," and "Love you," and Grandma and Grandpa are there. But I don't know too many families that are actually like that. I think that's a fantasy world that makes more people cry at Christmas than anything else.

Q: Do you think that's important for young people to know?

E: That the Waltons aren't real? And the Brady Bunch? Sure. Real families are not like that. One thing that depicts a real family for me—and that I work to get in a family— is this: Do they eat supper together? Eating together—not just a time when the family gets together and talks about what went wrong during the day, or Daddy holds forth on the bills—but sharing. You don't know how many families I get who never eat together. The young person makes his own supper. Or takes it in the TV room. Or the parents don't get home till late.

It takes two people to make a real family. And they can be any two people. But they must have a sense of family and commitment. Some people don't know what that is. They don't know the rituals that make a family—ways of observing holidays or each other's birthdays.

A young man was talking to me about his girlfriend's family, about how they fight—the mother and daughter really go at it. But he made this wonderful observation about how they resolve fights. They know how to get out of it and through it—the fights aren't helpless.

I think therapists are guilty of making it seem like you have to come to us to find out how to make a family work. But it shouldn't be a mystery that families get dysfunctional when they get either child-centered or parent-centered. There are things as basic as this: Families ought to be eating together. It shouldn't be threatening that a young person can make suggestions to an adult, just as an adult can make suggestions to a kid. We give and take, both. It has to be something like a seesaw. I know it's a terribly overused word—but it's *communication* that has to be established.

Again, if we're looking back on those earliest stages in a family, I wonder what the prognosis would be if we could try to help a child develop a sense of humor and joy in those first two years. I wonder how many of them would be suicides who had learned early on to develop laughter and a wry sense of humor when things don't go well. I see the difference in little ones—those who have temper tantrums and those who can laugh when things don't go well.

Q: But can you teach a sense of humor? Doesn't the laughter come from a sense of security?

E: Yes, but you have to have some example of someone being able to laugh at a hard time.

I think the whole issue of trust goes back to infancy.

Q: But what about kids who have nothing solid and secure in their backgrounds?

E: I see kids that I call invulnerable, and maybe there's a lesson there. For instance, I see kids whose mothers were in jail when they were born, and they immediately began the foster home shuffle. While they'll certainly always have missed something, among them there are survivors. The difference I find is in their ability to reach out to others. To find a teacher or a scout leader or coach or school nurse, or any of a lot of people—parents of friends, for example. It's the ones who still have their arms out who can make it.

When we see drawings from children, some children don't put arms on a body. That tells you something very strong about the ability to reach out. Then there are the ones who not only put on fingers—but fingers that are way long and tapered and that are just going to stretch out and reach as far as they can go.

I remember working with one kid who wanted something from an absentee father. And the point there was: Don't ask the people who aren't there for you. Don't keep looking for something from those who can't give it. Look for it where you can get it.

So the survivor kids, whether they're the children of alcoholics or children of parents who can't raise them, the invulnerable kids, the ones who may pay a price but will make it, are the ones who can find substitute people in their lives who will give them nurture, caring, sharing. It may be a series of people.

Q: What do you mean by invulnerable?

E: By invulnerable I mean those who are not going to get hurt. Vulnerable kids are going to stand in the rain and get a cold. The invulnerable kids aren't. And they have become invulnerable because they have found some way to cope with their own reality. They've become invulnerable to the harsh aloneness and lack of nurture that fate has dealt them. They do this by becoming survivors, by finding someone here and someone there. By reaching out.

I have a friend, raised in an orphanage till she was five, who has just given birth to her child—the first living relative she will ever know. In parenting, she is reparenting herself. In the ability to nurture and care, she recalls the one person in the orphanage who was special to her—who would take her food shopping, and who gave her a sense of being loved and special. Even with the loneliness of the orphanage, and the terrible disruption in her life, being adopted when she was five, she does have that ability to reach out.

For any of us, it's not a case of never being under stress. It's a case of what the solutions are. There are bad solutions. And there are good solutions.

It is hopeful to know that there *are* good solutions to some serious problems facing young people today, and that some of those "good" solutions are relatively easy to attain.

One ought to look for nurturing and caring where it can be found, for example. As was pointed out, sometimes the working through of a problem has to be: Don't look for it where you can't get it; look for it from those who can give it to you.

Is it too much to conjecture that if teens had other nurturing, caring places available to them when the family process broke down, that rather than turn to suicide as a way out, they might turn to others who could help? Is it naive to think that if there were school programs available, places and people to turn to when things got bleak, teens would resort less often to self-destructive methods of crying for help?

One of the most fundamental suggestions here was that families themselves could provide one of the antidotes to suicide. That families ought to share certain things— meals, celebrations of birthdays, family rituals. Certainly this is not a novel suggestion, but it is worth repeating. The ability to feel a part of a nurturing, caring unit is funda- mental to anyone's well-being, teen as well as adult. It takes two people to be a family—but they can be *any* two people. It may be that a teen who is in a terrible situation in a family might find nurturing with any one other family member— a brother or sister or perhaps a grandparent.

Certainly it is helpful to know that all of us can get way out on the far ends of the spectrum, but to know also that we can get back to that "comfort zone." For that speaks of hope. Yes, things can get tough. Yes, things can seem hopeless. But if we find someone and then reach out to that person—like the children who draw long fingers and arms in their pictures—if we reach out to one who *is* there for us, then we will not be so vulnerable to despair.

Chapter 10

Epilogue

Preventing Youth Suicide

It seems, as I come to the end of this book, that there is still so much left unsaid. The very questions I asked when I began still beg for answers: What has caused this upsurge in youth suicide? And what can be done to prevent it?

Some researchers cite as influencing factors the disintegration of the family due to the increase in divorce; the lack of stability in the home caused by the necessity of having two working parents; or the problems of the modern nuclear family with its lack of an extended support system. The increase in family violence, the sense of rootlessness caused by our mobile society, and the individual youth's lack of a clear sense of importance in the family have all been cited.

Other professionals remain unconvinced that the problems reside solely in the homes. The threat of nuclear war is mentioned by some as an influencing factor, as is the sense of helplessness engendered by that threat. There are more young people competing for fewer jobs. Many feel that the increase in the availability and use of drugs and alcohol is a prime contributing factor.

In my own interviews, I found some young people citing a sense of helplessness and worthlessness, of hopelessness and loneliness and isolation that drove them to attempt to end their own lives. Yet there were others who felt entirely different pressures—such things as the pressure to succeed, with success being measured by somebody else's standards. There were still others who spoke with great honesty about feelings of rage—the "I'll get them" feelings—that, while not acted upon, were present in their lives. And so, in all those interviews, I found the same thing that researchers are finding: that one cannot say that there is *a single* cause of youth suicide. Certain thoughts and urges to self-destruction may be similar. But each individual is unique, as each one's sadness and despair are unique.

I realize that certain aspects about youth suicide remain uncovered in this book. I did not, for example, quote directly from some of the major researchers in the field— although I've read and researched seemingly hundreds of books and articles on the subject and listened to an apparently equal number of tapes, and I've spoken directly with some of the experts involved.

While these scholarly people and articles and books certainly influenced my thoughts, as well as the thrust of my questions to young people, I did not include them directly. I am not a researcher, nor can I report on the research in the scholarly manner it deserves. In recording the people's stories here, I felt much more like a reporter. My interests, and perhaps my skills, are better tuned to reporting what those who are involved on a different level have to say—those who are the real victims of suicide, perhaps.

In addition, I did not attempt to cover the proliferation of programs in the schools today that are meant to deal with teen suicide. The programs are many, and so varied in content and scope that it would have been impossible to include them all. Most of the programs are so new that it is much too early to make assessments. I leave that for the educators courageously facing up to the challenge of helping their students deal with the issues of life and death.

What is the prognosis for youths who have attempted suicide? Can they go on to lead healthy, full lives? Or will they make further, more lethal attacks upon themselves? Again, the response to that is as unique as the individual. Yes, sadly, some will try again. Having failed the first or second time, they may, indeed, succeed. For some, nothing that anyone can do will prevent it.

But for many others who have made attempts on their lives, life will go on, and it will go on richer and fuller than before. Having faced what most of us do not have to face until we are much older—our own mortality—they have come back with courage and strength to help themselves. And to help others.

Finally, I believe that we can indeed prevent youth suicide. Not all suicides, no. And each death is, and will continue to be, a tragedy. But as a society, we have the power to make great strides toward prevention. That power resides in each of us—not surprisingly, perhaps, particularly in the hands of the young. Throughout this book and throughout the interviews and hundreds of conversations with youths and their families, I heard again and again, in different ways, in different words, the same message: if only someone were listening. If only someone knew.

And so I believe that suicide can be prevented—if the potential victim is recognized. But we must know the warning signs, we must hear and respond to the silent and often confused cries for help. Because this is one issue on which almost everyone agrees: Hear what youth is saying. Hear and respond. And lives can, and will, be saved.

Selected Bibliography

Alper, Joseph. "Depression At An Early Age." *Science 86,* May 1986, 45–50.

Alvarez, A. *The Savage God.* New York: Random House, 1970.

Bergson, Lisa. "Suicide's Other Victims." *The New York Times,* November 14, 1982.

Bettelheim, Bruno. *Surviving and Other Essays.* New York: Vintage Books, Random House, 1980.

Bolton, Iris. *My Son, My Son.* Atlanta: Bolton Press, 1983.

The Cambridge Hospital Department of Psychiatry and The Cambridge Hospital Center for the Study of Suicide. *Adolescent Suicide: Understanding and Responding.* Audiotapes from symposium. Boston and Los Angeles, 1986.

Cantor, Pamela. "The Effects of Youthful Suicide on the Family." *Psychiatric Opinion,* Volume 12, Number 6, July 1975, 6–11.

Chiles, John. *Teenage Depression and Suicide.* New York, New Haven, Philadelphia: Chelsea House Publishers, 1986.

Colt, George Howe. "The Painful Riddle of Teen Suicide." *Seventeen,* April 1985, 184–187, 221–222.

Farber, Maurice L. *Theory of Suicide.* New York: Funk and Wagnalls, 1968.

Giffin, Mary. "A Cry for Help: Teen Suicide." *Family Circle,* August 3, 1983, 28, 32–34, 68–69.

Giffin, Mary, and Carol Felsenthal. *A Cry for Help.* Garden City and New York: Doubleday and Company, 1983.

Grollman, Earl A., ed. *Suicide: Prevention, Intervention, Postvention.* Boston: Beacon Press, 1971.

Hendin, Herbert. *Suicide in America.* New York and London: W. W. Norton and Company, 1982.

———. *Black Suicide.* New York and London: Basic Books, Inc., 1969.

Joan, Polly. *Preventing Teenage Suicide.* New York: Human Sciences Press, 1985.

Klagsbrun, Francene. *Too Young to Die.* Boston: Houghton Mifflin and Company, 1976.

Kliman, Ann S. *Crisis.* New York: Holt, Rinehart and Winston, 1978.

Kübler-Ross, Elisabeth. *On Children and Death.* New York: Macmillan Publishing Company, 1983.

Leo, John. "Could Suicide be Contagious?" *Time,* March 6, 1986, 59.

Menninger, Karl Augustus. *Man against Himself.* New York: Harcourt, Brace, 1938.

Moffat, Mary Jane, ed. *In the Midst of Winter: Selections from the Literature of Mourning.* New York and Toronto: Vintage Books, Random House, 1982.

Reynolds, David K., and Norman Farberow. *Suicide: Inside and Out.* Berkeley, Los Angeles, London: University of California Press, 1976.

Rofes, Eric E., ed. *The Kids' Book about Death and Dying.* Boston and Toronto: Little, Brown and Company, 1985.

Ross, Charlotte. *Suicide in Youth and What You Can Do about It.* Pamphlet prepared by the Suicide Prevention and Crisis Center of San Mateo County, California, n.d.

Scarf, Maggie. *Unfinished Business*. Garden City and New York: Doubleday and Company, 1980.

Shneidman, Edwin S. *Suicide Thoughts and Reflections, 1960–1980*. New York: Human Sciences Press, 1981.

Spoonhour, Anne. "Teen Suicide." *People,* February 18, 1985, 76–78, 83.

U.S. Centers for Disease Control. *Morbidity and Mortality Weekly Report*, Volume 34, Number 24, June 21, 1985.

U.S. Department of Health and Human Services. *Youth Suicide,* n.d.

Viorst, Judith. *Necessary Losses*. New York: Simon and Schuster, 1986.

White-Bowden, Susan. *Everything to Live For*. New York: Poseidon Press, 1985.

INDEX